ARIS GATAS

CLAUDIO
RANIERI
T(H)INKERMAN

Meyer & Meyer Sport

Original title: Claudio Raineri – The Thinkerman
© Aris Gatas, arisgatas@yahoo.gr

Translation: Vagenas Alex

British Library Cataloguing in Publication Data
A catalogue record for this book is available from the British Library

Claudio Ranieri: T(h)inkerman
Maidenhead: Meyer & Meyer Sport (UK) Ltd., 2018
ISBN 978-1-78255-128-7

All rights reserved, especially the right to copy and distribute, including the translation rights. No part of this work may be reproduced–including by photocopy, microfilm or any other means–processed, stored electronically, copied or distributed in any form whatsoever without the written permission of the publisher.

© 2018 by Meyer & Meyer Sport (UK) Ltd.
Aachen, Auckland, Beirut, Budapest, Cairo, Cape Town, Dubai, Hägendorf, Indianapolis, Maidenhead, Singapore, Sydney, Tehran, Vienna

Member of the World Sport Publishers' Association (WSPA) www.w-s-p-a.org
Printed by CPI – Clausen & Bosse, Leck, Germany
ISBN 978-1-78255-128-7
E-Mail: info@m-m-sports.com
www.m-m-sports.com

Claudio Ranieri

CONTENTS

Introduction viii

1 "Nessun Dorma": My Life 1

2 Treat the Team As If It Were Your Child 8

3 An Endless Adventure 13

4 Sven's Shadow and Roman 17

5 Destiny Is Dancing 22

6 Leave With Dignity Even If You're Being Treated Unfairly 26

7 Accountants Worldwide Unite 31

8 The Charter Breaks Down En Route to the Mundial 38

9 Kings in England and Europe: Driven Away From Greece 44

10 Excuse Me, Sirs…Who Is the President? 50

11 Bombs Falling Everywhere 56

12 Left in the Dark 68

13 Unsuccessful Attempts 73

14 Greece Was My Mistake 76

15	The Metamorphosis of the Tinkerman	84
16	Ranieri Versus Mourinho	90
17	On the Road to a Miracle	98
	August 2015: Against All Odds From Day One	99
	September 2015: You Old Fox	101
	October 2015: Welcome, Thinkerman	103
	November 2015: Bionic Jamie	106
	December 2015: Dilly Ding Dilly Dong!	107
	January 2016: Claudio Got His Gun	111
	February 2016: Happy Days	112
	March 2016: Like Obama and Castro	115
	April 2016: Tears of a Lifetime	117
	May 2016: A Mother's Blessing	120
18	Leicester's Numbers	122
19	The Ranieri Sausage	129
20	The Legend of King Richard III and the Supernatural Title Win	133
21	Claudio's Magic Wand	141
22	Hello, Sharks, Welcome to the Funeral	150
23	How Things Change	157
24	Leicester's Market Value	178
25	The Algerian Magician	185

Contents

26 Jamie's Fairytale 192

27 You're Always Talking 200

28 Forrest Gump of Leicester 204

29 Morgan the Magic Rum 207

30 Ranieri Merchandise..210

31 Leicester Crisps 214

32 All Great Loves Go to Heaven 216

33 The Betting Miracle 222

34 The Man That Changed Our Lives 228

35 The Premier League Will Never Be the Same 232

36 Graffiti for Claudio 236

37 The Impersonator of Love....................................239

38 Don't Bite Off More Than You Can Chew..............241

39 Buddhist Monks and the Secret...........................247

40 The Magician From Thailand 251

41 Thailand: An Opening in Asia.............................258

42 Vichai and Leicester..263

43 Almond Sweets From Mykonos 266

44 The Thinkerman of Our Lives 269

INTRODUCTION

In early May of 2016, followers of the global sports scene had just one question in mind: How did Ranieri manage to become king of the Premier League?

This eleven-word question coincides with the greatest miracle that has ever taken place in the world of football teams. A team and a coach who had been nearly forgotten a year earlier had ultimately achieved the impossible by claiming the title of the toughest league on the planet.

Everyone began to realize that something was changing for Leicester some time before the miracle even occurred.

In the magical world of English football, this is not the first time that a Cinderella has become queen; Kenny Dalglish had achieved something similar with Blackburn in 1994-1995.

However, it is the first time in the history of the sport that the entire football world wanted this Cinderella to take the throne. And it wanted this to happen because her prince, Claudio Ranieri, and his knights had, in their own inimitable fashion, initiated the entire football kingdom into the cult of his Cinderella.

Before winning the title, Blackburn made a record transfer by acquiring Alan Shearer, and spent huge sums in order to get that extra push. Ranieri's Leicester had a budget that was even lower than Sunderland's and Watford's but her story had the fairytale ending it deserved, as anyone who fully embraced the spirit of this team knew that it would. It became a symbol for faith and

Introduction

the right to dream about life, work, and day-to-day reality, simply by doing it in her own way, guided by optimism and fellowship among players. One for all and all for their leader.

It did not take long for that leader to gain recognition and this is Ranieri's greatest achievement. This is the message he created by following his path and maintaining his attitude. There is a sense of dignity and honesty in everything that he does, both within and apart from Leicester. He remained goal-oriented throughout his own journey of self-improvement and self-fulfillment in the world of English football; he went from being the Tinkerman with Chelsea in 2004 to becoming the Thinkerman with Leicester in 2016.

His confidence and devotion became known to all parts of the world, his infectious positive energy lifting the spirits of many and sending one single message: that we too can reach out and touch a miracle, even when it seems that all odds are against us.

Over the last two years, I met and interviewed Claudio Ranieri during the two most crucial moments of his coaching career. The first during the lowest—we met shortly before his catastrophic experience coaching the Greek National Team, on the eve of the game against the Faroe Islands—and the latter at his most glorious—a few weeks before he was crowned King of the Premier League. He was exactly the same: a man with a plan and a very structured way of thinking. Only his emotions, so clearly etched on his face, were different; peaceful in Leicester, horrified by the defeat in Rome.

He remains a true gentleman, principled and direct in both thought and speech. A balanced man, unwavering in his ideas.

CLAUDIO RANIERI – T(H)INKERMAN

It took two years to go from abject sorrow to utter joy; from complete doubt to universal acceptance. Life plays strange games and Claudio Ranieri's journey over the last two years was one of them.

The book you hold in your hands is a record of the stories from those whose lives have been touched by Ranieri's miracle with Leicester, from the players to the Thai tycoon who owns the British team; from his close associates to Peter, the Italian pizza man who saw his life change since Ranieri started treating his squad to pizza after every match they were not scored against; from local small businessmen to the street vendors outside the King Power Stadium.

It can be seen as a young persons' guide to the strange world of football. From Ranieri's adventure they can learn that nothing is impossible when you keep the faith, have willpower, and are committed in all you do. It contains previously unpublished accounts of the Italian coach's course over the last two years and of coincidences that almost border on the supernatural. It's a thrilling story full of imagination and excitement but also his characteristic modesty: from the experience of crushing defeat to conquering the Premier League and eventually ultimate recognition for a man who performed miracles after having experienced disappointment on the bench of another team.

This man, who brought happiness to all those around him and gained the highest seal of approval, is Claudio. An honorable man now worshiped in every part of the world for his originality and diversity all the way from the small town of Leicester to Bangkok, Rome, Athens, and New York.

Introduction

His own success has inspired people to believe in themselves, attain their own goals, and see life in a different light. He made people happy with the miracle of Leicester City yet he has always remained genuine. Never for even a moment did he let his newfound glory change him. He has remained confident and wise and consistently creative. A daring but conscientious man with the effortless grace of a British noble. He has provided an example worth following by all those who aspire to reach the top.

It is not an easy task to assess all of Ranieri's achievements from the last two years in a concrete fashion. Something new always arises, no matter how many things one discovers. With his trademark positivity he was able to effect the transformation of an objectively negative experience into a miracle. However, his story is not just about the miracle itself that had the world's attention transfixed on the football scene, it is also about his ability to alter the perception of the sport itself. His story epitomizes the victory of all those who really struggle to accomplish what they desire at some point in their lives.

From July 25, 2014, when the official announcement was made that he would be coaching the national team of Greece, until the time Leicester conquered the Premier League, Ranieri had been on an upward journey. Through the stories of those who were around him during that time—those whose lives he changed—we learn that he was always the key. He is given credit for the greatest part of their success.

The international media presented the miracle of Leicester as one of 2016's most amazing moments. Everyone set out to discover the secret of his success. Ranieri achieved the unexpected because he didn't work in stereotypical ways. He thought outside of the box in such a way that he was able to fire up his players' belief in themselves. The established perception and image of English football was completely turned on its head during the 2015-2016 season.

The teams of the Premier League implement specific tactics in order to reach the top. Money is the driving force. He knew this well from his experience on the benches of other great teams, where he had managed huge budgets. When it came to managing Leicester, he knew that he was taking the risk of following practices, which, in different times, may not have allowed him to remain on the bench of a Premier League club for a long time.

He immediately agreed to keep on the previous coach's associates and only brought his fitness trainer with him. This was his first internal victory. He collaborated with people he had never met before. He was recommended several assistants and had to figure out right away who was really going to be of value to him, thus saving precious time.

He never disturbed his new team's daily equilibrium; instead, he followed the regimen that had been established by his predecessors because he was reluctant to risk anything by making drastic changes. He knew that by keeping the key links of the chain intact, he would be able to make it stronger. He allowed his mind to think freely and never imprisoned it within traditional, conventional ideas and solutions like those taught in coaching schools. Ranieri stepped outside the ordinary and worked with what he learned from experience. He trusted his instincts.

The players were given two days off per week so they could unwind after the intense matches. During the season, they were given a week off so that they could go on holiday. People thought

Introduction

he was insane and judged him for this decision. The usual strategy in professional football leagues is to literally not give the players any room to catch a breath. They are put through double and triple training sessions throughout the season and are expected to perform like robots. Ranieri's players were just regular people. Athletes with their ups and downs. Ranieri bucked the system by applying innovative strategies. This could have been his downfall, but things turned out otherwise.

As a matter of fact, taking that risk led to celebration later. He chose freedom and authenticity and did not restrict himself to established rules, even in seemingly little things, which made all the difference in the end. He did so with sensitivity and trust in his beloved players.

Displaying his trademark maturity and responsibility, he did not attempt to force them to follow a strict diet when they went home. He gave each player the freedom to choose their own meals. He trusted their own judgement, and they returned that trust. He gave them freedom in their choices every step of the way of their great journey together.

Every year, the top European teams invest a vast amount of money in nutrition programs. It is a serious and important factor for the players' well-being and performance. The Leicester City team did not eat junk food at motorway service stations like Jamie Vardy had to do in his childhood. They all adequately followed their Italian coach's method of self-improvement. Everyone was personally responsible for their own actions and he urged them to rely on their willpower and absolute commitment to reach their goal. Everyone was their own dietitian, nutritionist, and physiotherapist, all rolled into one.

CLAUDIO RANIERI – T(H)INKERMAN

This was a great victory for Ranieri. The greatest before all the victories that were to come on the pitch. It was a gamble and a life lesson for all of them. An example worth following. When driven by passion and a thirst to succeed, people can achieve anything if they put their heart and soul in whatever they do by focusing on their goal and thinking positively.

In the history of sport and British football specifically, Claudio Ranieri will be remembered like another Leonidas of Sparta, who, together with a small band of warriors, achieved the impossible.

1

"Nessun Dorma": My Life

The chanting and cheers of Leicester's ecstatic supporters echo through King Power Stadium as they all euphorically celebrate winning the Premier League title. It is a fascinating sight. To the west of the stadium's main entrance, one-man skiffs gliding noiselessly along the water of the River Soar, as if rowing in time to the music of celebration, create a dreamlike scene.

Hordes of rowdy Leicester supporters hurry to catch the last performance of the season. The festive atmosphere in the stadium blends perfectly with all the decorations. A huge makeshift podium filled with flowers stands at centerfield. Everything is ready.

When Claudio calmly raises his left hand to signal the crowd to hush, everyone is perplexed. He does not do that often. He usually does the opposite, waving both arms in the air wildly in a circular motion, calling upon the crowd to boost the team's moral. This time it is different. This time it is magical.

He is the champion of England and Andrea Bocelli is serenading him with his spellbinding voice. This is exactly what he has dreamed about for many years. Indeed, this is like a scene taken from a movie. In fact, the last two years of his life have indeed been a movie with himself cast as both the star and an extra. There is nothing else quite like this.

The fans settle down, instinctively responding to Claudio's request. He has never refused them anything. Now it is time for them to reciprocate. With his other hand, just moments ago, Ranieri led his blind friend, Andrea Bocelli, to the specially designed stage on centerfield.

Today is his day. This is the moment that changed the status of world football. Even the most football-ignorant person on the planet can comprehend what this win means. Leicester—up until yesterday only an insignificant English team—has been crowned queen.

The image of Ranieri and Bocelli standing next to each other fills the screens. People are celebrating in Bangkok and crying proud tears of joy in his birthplace, Testaccio. The celebration of Leicester winning the title is one of the most powerful moments in the history of the Premier League. Words cannot describe how unique this moment is. Andrea Bocceli came to Leicester from Rome in honor of his friend Claudio.

Andrea is wearing a Leicester jersey with his name printed on the back. He has been unable to see since childhood; he paid for his passion for the sport with his eyesight. At the age of twelve, he went to play football with his mates in his small Italian neighborhood. A strong blow to the head with the ball was fatal to his already ailing eyes. For years, he had been suffering from glaucoma, but doctors would later tell his parents that the ball striking his head sealed the fate of the boy's sight.

God may have deprived him of his sight, but he gave the world the joy of enjoying Bocelli's divine voice. And this divine voice had come to King Power Stadium as Ranieri's special guest, on the finest day of his football career.

Bocelli bursts into song. Magical melodies fill the stadium and it seems as if angels are floating upon the grass of the pitch.

The boisterous Leicester fans are not easily disciplined so their commotion is overshadowing the moment of Bocelli's performance. They are all united, living the dream. It is not easy to tame thousands of people. They are delirious. Claudio turns his head to look at Andrea and lifts his left hand signaling to the people that the moment is crucial.

He motions them to pause for a moment, so they can all listen and embark on a journey out of this world together, with the tenor guiding the way. Bocelli's rendition of "Nessun Dorma" now fills the air.

For the second time, Claudio is introducing the fans to something they certainly have not experienced before. The first was the championship win. Now he is asking the crowd to show their guest, who has come there to join them in celebrating victory, the respect and attention he deserves. This gesture is indicative of Ranieri's character. He has shown how he thinks and how he experiences the moment. He has done so several times throughout the year when facing his opponents.

The fans abruptly fall silent and stand listening, mesmerized. The two Italians on stage leave everyone speechless. Claudio closes his eyes and fights back the tears, all of his emotions wrapped in the magic of the moment. It is his day. In his mind, he watches the film of the last two years of his life unfold. He travels even further back, from his father's butcher shop in Testaccio to the principality of Monaco. The thoughts, feelings, tears of an emotional man. All one inside him.

This day is for his players and for the fans who believed in the miracle and supported him with their love the entire season, and who had been there for him during crucial moments when he called out for their help.

Like on a wet evening at King Power, in the middle of March 2016, against Newcastle, the match where Okazaki scored by leaping like a ninja for an overhead kick, putting Leicester City in the lead. It was an incredible goal! Defeating Newcastle was imperative for Leicester, who had eight matches to go until the season finale. Claudio knew this well, but had noticed how tired his players were growing. A few days earlier, Newcastle had welcomed their new manager, Rafa Benitez, and the Spanish coach, smart and level-headed, was ready for the best, but also prepared for the worst.

The clock ticked and Newcastle picked up their pace. Ranieri, sensing the change in the opponent, resorted to a tactic that always worked. He turned to the fans and threw his fists in the air, imploring them to motivate their team. As if they had received an electric shock, forty thousand frantic fans got up and cheered enthusiastically, pushing their team with their positive energy. A wave of faith spread through King Power. All became one, the fans, the players, and their maestro who had given them the cue.

After that, it had not been necessary for Ranieri to do anything out of the ordinary against Newcastle besides some standard substitutions; his job was done. Leicester defeated Newcastle 1-0, got the golden three points, and now had—weeks in advance—their eye on the prize.

In life, one cannot demand to be respected. The lesson to be learned here is that respect is earned. This was clearly demonstrated by the way the crowd responded to the coach's signal. The forty thousand people urging their team in unison during the game with Newcastle, are the same crowd that now stands silent in front of Bocelli, respecting Ranieri's signal. They listen to the music and travel with Claudio, who has become their ringleader. He is the perfect guide and leader, having total control over everyone: forty thousand people and his twenty-five players.

As things would have it, he was able to pull through in the end and accomplish everything he wanted to do in his career. It had been an incredible adventure full of twists and emotions: from a difficult start with Cagliari—where his managerial career began—to the crushing moment of the Greek national team's defeat by the Faroe Islands. There had been remarkable moments with top European football clubs. There had been the magical nights with his beloved Roma, with Valencia, and the principality of Monaco. Abramovich and Chelsea, which he had adored. Magical Madrid and Atletico, Florence too. Two years with Napoli.

It is story like a novel with its ups and downs. He, however, always remained dapper, Italian to the core, sitting on Leicester's bench with his lucky tie and black coat.

The story of the black cashmere coat seems almost supernatural. Almost every match was won when he wore that coat. It seemed like he was fated to wear that coat every time there was a big match in the 2015-2016 season. This coat is destined for a prominent place in a sports museum.

All people face good and bad moments in their lives and it has been the same for Ranieri; the road of his coaching career was not covered in rose petals. That would not have been the case anyway. The signs were there that things were working against him even before he took his place on Leicester's bench on July 13, 2015. It was not only because of his disastrous collaboration with the national Greek team, but because those who welcomed him at Leicester—chiefly Gary Lineker—did not think it was a good time for him to take over the team. It was not because they did not believe him to be a great manager or because things had not gone well with another team prior to the move. The problem was timing, which made even the most optimistic of them skeptical about it.

Leicester was just coming out of a long stint with a manager that had become synonymous with the club, and that was none other than Nigel Pearson. Nowhere in the world do teams trust their managers as much as the British teams do their own. Perhaps the greatest difficulty facing a successor on a team's bench is having to weather the storm in order to be able to achieve longevity.

Not every day could be a happy day and he often had to be hard on his players during pre-season training.

Sometimes he even used military training methods, although, as with every team he worked with, he treated all the athletes fairly. He gave them many opportunities and brought out the best of themselves. He was often warm and attentive, at other times dynamic and ruthless, while always having the common interest at heart, always exhibiting positive energy and team spirit.

After the game against Everton at the finale of a historical year, and just before he appeared in front of the reporters in the press conference, Claudio put on one of the most expensive suits he owned. The occasion called for it because he was the champion of England and, as a true Italian, he had to look sharp.

Italians tend to be very stylish. They will wake up in the morning and before they do anything else, they will put on their cologne and choose a tie for the day. Ranieri likes to look smart and wear expensive clothes. He is a man of exquisite taste.

He also knows how to embrace the moment. Every moment, especially one such as this. Standing next to Andrea Bocelli, "Nessun Dorma" soaring through the stadium, with his eyes closed, his life and memories floated through his mind.

2

Treat the Team As If It Were Your Child

The battle cries at the end of World War II filled the European continent as the Chinese and South Korean forces took over Seoul in the early 1950s. During the same era, Bell Laboratories creates the first telephone answering machine, changing people's lives forever. The Stasi, the secret police founded in East Germany, will change the political and social sphere for many years to come. In Silverstone, England, the first round of the Formula 1 world championship takes place and alters the history of auto racing, while in Cape Canaveral Air Force Station, the first rocket is launched. On October 26, 1951, exactly six days after Ranieri's birth, Winston Churchill becomes Britain's prime minister once again.

Rome lives in the present by using the past in the same way someone would use old tools. Rome now has to heal its own wounds following the end of the interwar years.

As Claude Moatti says, the ancient dimension of Rome is present everywhere in the city, even floating on the waters of Tiber, where the ancient remains of the Ponte Rotto—the oldest stone bridge in Rome—still stand.

Ruins of the past, beauty upon beauty, take on new shapes and forms, even if they are sometimes incongruous.

During the Middle Ages, there were residential buildings atop the ruins of the Theatre of Marcellus and the thermal public baths of Diocletian were turned into a church designed by Michelangelo. Again in the Middle Ages, the triumphal arches, theaters, and tombs were converted into fortresses or towers, while the markets and the Colosseum were used as marble quarries. The Christians did not look down upon the pagan temples, so they moved into them like conquerors taking the homes of the defeated, dumbfounded by the beauty of these buildings.

The surrounding areas outside the museums are filled with ruins. In many places they extend along public streets, and sometimes they are enclosed in the national gardens where someone can enjoy them when they go to see the wild animals in the zoos. They are at Via Appia, in Colle Oppio, in front of the Villa Medici, below the churches and the houses. Rome stirs and awakens, and all of the city's ancient figures stand before you like characters in a three-dimensional picture book.

All of Rome's history can be studied through this resurrection of ancient times as if it were a monumental fossil preserving the remnants of ancient hippodromes and theaters throughout the city. The past resurfaces and you can sense the grace of times gone by all around you.

Today, one is used to the busy medieval streets, with the younger population in helmets zipping through traffic on motor scooters. Rome, an enchanting interwar city which was thought to have died, is still very much alive and living through its ancient history. A place like no other, the past constantly co-exists with the present, creating an eternal city.

In Testaccio, there are elegant white housing complexes that recall the dynamism of the beginning of the century. A country road passes through the old slaughterhouses, which today have become a cultural center. The road winds past stables with horse-drawn carriages for tourists, and ends at a space where there are carriages that are no longer used.

In this working-class district in the Italian capital, Claudio Ranieri was born on October 20, 1951. It was a neighborhood that didn't have the best reputation, but it was also a neighborhood where children aimed to continue the family trade for their future profession. Here, at the banks of the Tiber, young Claudio grew up having only one dream the first years of his life: to be a butcher just like his father, whom he idolized.

The neighborhood was famous for its slaughterhouses, but the lads who lived there had just one goal in life, to escape and live the dream. It was not an easy life and seeing his father wake up early in the morning and return home late at night, young Claudio decided to rebel against his own destiny.

At first, football was just a game the neighborhood children played with a ball made of rags, but it later became a means for him to live out his own dream. When he walked through the threshold of Roma's Academies, his career in the fascinating world of football began. He had only one goal in mind, to reach the top and make his parents proud.

In the beginning he managed quite well, and even though all the kids his age admired the big top-scoring players like Mazzola and Rivera, Claudio chose to play as a defender. He had a more cerebral approach to the game, but he was also quick and decisive. He signed his first contract as a professional footballer for Roma.

For two seasons he had only six league appearances and he realized he might have to take a step back in order to breathe new life into his football career. He had a one-month loan spell with Siracusa from Roma, but his greatest moments were with Catanzaro, where he played for eight years and had two successful campaigns. He lived such moments with Catania as well, where he played for two years, and also with Palermo which was promoted to Serie A in the two-year period from 1984 to 1986.

Claudio's career as a player ended when he was 35 years old. Right away, the passion he had for coaching grew within him. Ever since he had donned his player's uniform, he was like a second coach on the pitch.

"The team is like a child. If a child makes a mistake and you put them under pressure, a child cannot grow up to be confident."

This was his motto and it was embedded in his mind from the start. It became the strategy that later took him to the top. He believed that positive energy, patience, and persistence pay off in the end. These are things that never ceased to matter to him since the time he was on the bench of Vigor Lamezia, an amateur Italian team. It was these things that accompanied him to the Premier League championship.

Essentially, Ranieri's start in his incredible coaching career was with Puteolana, a small football club from Pozzuoli, founded in 1902, which joined the Italian Football Federation of Italy in 1914. In the early 1920s, Puteolana played in the Serie A, and won titles in the Serie C.

Claudio fell in love with coaching from the very first day. He started to look at the job from a different angle. The results were fantastic. Fifteen clubs and a national team! Through it all, he was passionate and devoted. Through it all, enthusiasm and productivity were never lacking. There were no exceptions to the rule. He faced everything with a smile and positive energy, even on the most difficult days.

Lamezia, Puteolana, Cagliari, Napoli, Fiorentina, Valencia (twice), Atletico Madrid, Chelsea, Parma, Juventus, Roma, Inter Milan, Monaco, the Greek National Team, Leicester...

"I want to coach even in the afterlife, which I do believe in," Claudio always says when expressing his love for his position on the benches.

3

An Endless Adventure

Claudio will always be passionate about his beliefs in all that he does. Just like his first great moment when he rocked the boat of Italian football with Cagliari. With consecutive promotions from the third division, he led them to Serie A. And if well begun is half done in most things in life, Ranieri could not have made his introduction to the world of football in a better way.

It was only natural that his name would become widely familiar outside the Italian border. His first important milestone was with the difficult Italian south, Napoli, in the post-Maradona era. In the two years he was with the Partenopei club, he was not able to get a title, but left as his legacy Gianfranco Zola, a player that he always appreciated and that he frequently mentions in his public statements. It was a gamble that paid off with Napoli, and he won more gambles of this kind throughout his coaching career.

It was a bumpy road and, even though the story did not have a happy ending, it left him with a legacy of experiences and life lessons. The collaboration ended with Napoli in fourth place in the Campionato. He was sacked by the owner, Corrado Ferlaino, who was an unusual man—in 2002, after Ranieri's dismissal, Ferlaino was arrested and sent to jail.

History records each person's story in its own mysterious way. Such is life, not only for football clubs. There is no escaping destiny.

Florence is a lovely place to go on holiday for its ambience, its beauty, and its romantic vibe! It is also famous for Fiorentina, the city's football team that has written its own history in the Campionato. It was the next challenge for the restless but always determined and always professional Claudio. He always wanted his choices to result in ideal collaborations. Fiorentina was looking for a coach with his qualities and Vittorio Cecchi Gori, an eccentric football club owner, immediately appointed him.

His destiny to be involved with eccentric people followed him there too. He stayed on the bench of the Viola for four years, working with great players like Batistuta. He did wonderful things with them, leading them through noteworthy victories and an Italian cup, as well as the Super Cup of 1995-1996.

There are moments in his coaching career when promoting great players was his main goal. At the end of the day, he enjoyed being able to bask in the results of his work, which he had set the conditions for.

When he took over Valencia in 1997, he knew exactly where he was going. He was to coach a team with the lowest scores. During his first stint, he managed to lead the team to win the Spanish Copa del Rey in 1999! The initiative to recruit new players from the academies, who later brought the club to the top, was very successful; it felt as if they had already won championships and cups together. Mendieta, Angulo, Farinos, and goalkeeper Santiago Canizares were his choices, players that he had been watching while they were still in academies or that he brought in as transfers from other teams and then promoted.

His training regimens are created with an eye to the future, not just short-term results. For 2015-2016, there was no possibility to get new players, although he was always in touch with all the coaches of all the clubs.

It is a known fact that life plays curious games, and Ranieri experienced this firsthand throughout his career.

After Valencia came the offer from Atletico Madrid, which was not without risk. The Spanish team had already entered a liquidation process due to debts of the owner, the eccentric Jesus Gil. Even before taking the position, Claudio knew that things would be working against him. Not only did he have to deal with the eccentric president of the Spanish team, he also had to face the prospect of demotion to the second division because of Atletico's low ranking. Gil was asking him to do impossible things and Claudio realized right away that he would have no future at Vicente Calderon, and he resigned before Gil could dismiss him. At the end of the 1999-2000 season, Atletico, with its many problems, was relegated from the Primera Division. But Claudio had nipped the situation in the bud, so there was no possibility for him to be considered a loser.

This was a lesson that he remembered beyond a shadow of a doubt: you must always listen to your heart and trust your instincts. Both his heart and his instincts were screaming inside him, telling him not to go to Madrid. But it happened and he took a hit, which he vowed to learn from. He began working on his ability to approach people with his personality. He became stellar in public relations. He is good at it because he acts from the heart. He has never deceived anyone, even though thousands of words have been written about the compensation he received after leaving some of the clubs. He made sure to work as a professional should.

When you meet Claudio Ranieri in person, you realize he is a man who oozes dignity. He does not do it pretentiously, and he is not putting on an act. He is acting as himself. This is the role that suits him the best.

Despite the fact that his career was not at its best after leaving Spain, he always had his charm to rely on. He knew how to polish and sell himself. There is no way he could ever fade into the background, because he knows how to read the moment and weigh the facts. So, it is only natural that his next team should be on the level he himself desired. But destiny had more adventures in store for him.

4

Sven's Shadow and Roman

Throughout Ranieri's entire coaching career, Chelsea had been one of his greatest loves. In the summer of 2000, when entering discussions with the Londoners, his only concern was that there would be a language barrier should they come to an agreement. Ranieri was 49 years old at the time and could not speak English well enough to communicate properly. He needed English lessons.

Upon arriving in London, he considered himself fortunate because Chelsea had Italian and Spanish players. In the beginning, since the players who could understand him interpreted his instructions to the rest, everyone knew what he was telling them. But Claudio believed that direct communication with his squad was imperative. He did not want his poor English skills to come between them.

So he hit the books and learned to speak English, even though the problem could have been solved with a professional interpreter. But he did not want that. He would need to have physical contact with the players (e.g., when taking their pulse) so he felt he needed to be able to communicate with them himself, maintaining complete control without the intervention of anyone else. He had to improve his knowledge of the English language.

CLAUDIO RANIERI – T(H)INKERMAN

He was off to an average start with Chelsea and not very pleased with himself. In the summer, he was asked to lower the budget for the transfers, a request which, in the big clubs, is equivalent to being half-dismissed.

The transfer market in the summer of 2011 had some exceptional players that would enable Chelsea to change its status. However, the Bosman ruling regarding the free movement of players caused the prices of those players who could really make a difference to skyrocket.

Ranieri wanted to rebuild Chelsea from scratch. His first move was to recruit Frank Lampard from West Ham, a player who was to become a legend at Stamford Bridge.

That year, Claudio invested almost all the transfer budget in the acquisition of William Gallas from Olympique Marseille. The sum of 35,000,000 EUR for the Frenchman was considered exorbitant by many.

But the Italian was well aware that in order for something to be built properly, you must start from the bottom and work your way up. He did exactly that by spending money to recruit a defender and not a high-profile center forward. The cases of Petit, Zenden, and Gronkjaer could be considered anything but supplementary, and Claudio expected many things from them. But the optimism and joy did not last for long. The move that would spoil the overall climate was soon to be made.

Many times, teams rely on their fans and the karma they create. Chelsea is such a team with enthusiastic fans from all over the world. A disruption of equilibrium can cause poor progress on a new endeavor.

What Ranieri attempted at the time was to refresh the team. Dennis Wise was an icon for Chelsea fans and the decision to sell him, in combination with Chelsea's poor results, created a climate of skepticism against Ranieri. Added to this was Chelsea's defeat against Arsenal in the FA Cup final, and placing sixth in the championship. There was an explosion of objections against him.

He received harsh criticism for many things, especially for the many player substitutions he would make during matches. The British media gave him the Tinkerman nickname because he would constantly change the lineup and tactics at any given time, from one game to the next.

Chelsea was very weak financially because of the team's poor performance. Claudio's future on the team's bench seemed uncertain. However, the team bounced back emphatically and secured a place in the Champions League after defeating Liverpool. Claudio recovered at the brink of complete and utter failure. It was like being given the kiss of life!

Even though things had not gone well as far as results were concerned, Ranieri had managed to sign new players to Chelsea. He was proud of players Samuele Dalla Bona and Mario Stanic and new talents John Terry, Robert Huth, and Carlton Cole during his stay in London.

When Roman Abramovich came into the picture, he brought a new perspective to the Chelsea football club, but from the very first day the Russian tycoon set foot there, Claudio remained uncertain. He had gone through a lot previously and the British media were constantly looking for the opportunity to set him up as the first easy target of the new season.

Everywhere in the world, imminent changes in a football club that stem from a new owner's decisions bring a breath of fresh air. Sometimes the results may not be desirable, but only the idea of a change can alter the players' attitudes. Claudio managed to always remain calm, sensible, and rational.

Abramovich offered him a large sum of money to manage Chelsea's new season, but it seemed as though Sven-Goran Eriksson's shadow constantly hovered overhead in the Stamford Bridge sky. Abramovich had met with the Swedish coach several times, and he would artfully let it be known that these meetings took place. It was his obvious way of putting Claudio under pressure. The Russian had already indicated who Ranieri's replacement would be, even before the Italian attempted anything. Apparently, the owner of Chelsea felt that this style of pressure would have a beneficial effect for the club at that time.

Sven-Goran Eriksson, manager of the England national football team, would dash to these meetings at Abramovich's request, putting even more pressure on Claudio. Although officially Chelsea officials denied that anything of the sort ever took place, scenarios for a possible takeover by Eriksson were written on a daily basis in 2003, so somebody was obviously adding fuel to the fire.

Claudio was not intimidated by this. Most importantly, he was not affected by any warning signs. The season was progressing better than ever, and the team performed well in many games. The defense was perfect, the best recorded thus far. Chelsea was scored against less than in any other season in the club's history.

David Platt knew the secrets of the Premier League and those of European football very well. As a sports commentator, there were few instances where he did not provoke reactions with his views.

When he mentioned Ranieri, he said, "Building a team that can win the title and actually steering this team to the title are two entirely different matters."

Platt's observation was a symbolic message concerning the way Ranieri should be operating during the challenging time on the bench of Chelsea. But he was also putting a label on him. At the end of the season, in May 2004, the termination of the agreement between Claudio and Abramovich's Chelsea was quietly announced. A year of scenarios, which raged on a daily basis, had gone by. Chelsea's interest in Eriksson was now fact. But, as we said before, life plays curious games.

In Portugal, a peculiar bloke with a strong personality—and rather self-centered—emerged on the global coaching map, making his presence known in his unique way. With the successes of Porto on a European level, Jose Mourinho had made the start. He would later write his own history in some of the biggest clubs in the world for many years to come.

Abramovich was delighted with Mourinho and his references. He liked the blasé attitude of "The Special One." He preferred him over Eriksson, so he gave him the keys to Chelsea. Ranieri left and was replaced by Mourinho. This was enough to intrigue everyone, especially the media, and everything that followed between the two men was like something out of a movie.

Many times in life, there are situations when people use the phrase "a wise man does not make the same mistake twice" and Claudio had faced this many times.

His second time passing through Valencia would be just as dramatic as his last term with Chelsea.

5

Destiny Is Dancing

Upon Claudio's return to the Mestalla, in June of 2004, he preferred to put his trust on players from the Campionato for his new endeavour. Fiore, Corradi, and Di Vaio were the strongest players Claudio persuaded to join him on his second venture.

At the beginning of the 2004-2005 season, Valencia was off to an impressive start. In the first matches, the team won at home and away, so they were able to stay on the top of the league tables. The team won the Super Cup against Porto as well. It seemed like the road ahead would indeed be strewn with rose petals.

October is the most crucial month of the year in all championships around the world. It is when the teams show what their potential is for the upcoming year. October 2004 was a gloomy month for Ranieri's Valencia with just one win in seven matches.

Disaster seemed to come full circle when midway through the Spanish championship, Valencia lost to Inter Milan with a score of 5-1. Valencia was automatically eliminated from the Champions League.

The dark clouds of distrust began to gather in the sky over the Mestalla Stadium. There never really was any substantial recovery from that. He found himself having to justify his actions regarding the transfers. He had taken full responsibility. At the same time, he received daily criticism for not using the Argentine attacking midfielder, Pablo Aymar. The sinister force behind his collaboration troubles was lurking in Valencia as well. "The Tinkerman fell flat on his face on his way to the Mestalla" was the grim epilogue for Ranieri's stint with Valencia.

The constant changes in the line-ups of the team, but also the tactics he used—something akin to what he was accused of with Chelsea—was the main reason he was sacked from the Valencia club. His dismissal was announced on February 25, 2005, after the elimination from the Champions League by Steaua Bucharest. Valencia was not in the cards for him. Destiny was not on his side for that team either.

Even before he left Valencia, he knew he had no future with a Spanish team. He received almost 3,000,000 GBP compensation pay for the premature termination of his contract with Valencia. The amount was the main topic of discussion for many days in Spain.

The famous controversy about Claudio Ranieri's compensations began around that time, and it's true that many times in the future the subject was overly discussed.

Any professional, no matter what sector they belong to, must be compensated for the damages rendered against them by the party with whom they have entered into an agreement. There are judicial disputes worldwide regarding financial transactions every day. The difference in Ranieri's case was that the amounts he was asking for were so large that they caused ordinary mortals' heads to spin. Such discussions about his compensation continued many times after his tenures had ended with Monaco, Juventus, and the national team of Greece.

Claudio returned to Rome needing only to relax. He was not willing to go back to the pressures of being on a bench of a football club right way. In previous years, things were very tense, mainly due to the pressure he had been put under. He had solved the problem of earning a livelihood and was determined that his next choice be well thought-out. He had gained experience with everything he did, but deep down he knew that he could have avoided many pitfalls.

He waited about a year and a half before making a move, and in February of 2007 he decided to become manager for Parma. It was one of the best milestones of his coaching career. Everyone agrees that the results were very impressive.

When he first arrived to the bench of the team, he was met with disarray. Parma's relegation was looming. Sometimes the statistical estimations of football teams or of the players themselves may not always be accurate. When it comes to the coaches of the teams, however, there is a greater and more powerful incentive to discuss the matter.

With Stefano Pioli on the bench of Parma, the team made 15 points in 23 matches in the Campionato. When Claudio Ranieri was appointed, however, the transformation in their overall performance was evident from the very next day. The team was defeated 1-0 by Sampdoria for his first match, but then he helped the team pick up 17 points in ten games. Parma was able to avoid relegation and finished 12th in the championship.

There were some impressive matches where the team played quite aggressively. A storm of enthusiasm broke out when the team scored three goals against Empoli and four against Messina. Claudio led the team to extraordinary results. He was again the most popular coach on the Italian benches. He was sought after by Manchester City, Fulham, Palermo, Juventus, and even Roma.

All the signs were there that he had come full circle in his short duration with Palma. He proved that he was a great coach. His mentality on the benches guided him to act at the right time and with his heart. All eyes were upon him worldwide.

6

Leave With Dignity Even If You're Being Treated Unfairly

The Calciopolis scandal did not just shake up the Italian football scene, it provoked reactions worldwide as well when, in 2006, the Italian police brought a match-fixing scandal to light.

Recorded telephone conversations were presented uncovering a network between leading football figures and referees, whose main intention was to alter the results of the Italian championship games. Famous Italian clubs were involved in the scandal, like Juventus, Milan, Fiorentina, and Lazio. This caused an uproar, resulting in all the teams involved being relegated into lower divisions.

The Old Lady had returned to Serie A in the summer of 2007 and was seeking a coach. Ranieri was considered the most suitable to clean up the team, set it straight on the road to success, and make it whole again.

On June 4, 2007, the Italian press wrote about Ranieri sealing the deal with Juventus. The next day it was world news. He signed a three-year contract with Juventus, which was to commence on July 1, 2007. Though there were some reactions none was intense enough to cause the cancellation of the partnership.

Leave With Dignity Even If You're Being Treated Unfairly

True to his habit of signing some of the best players the moment he set foot in a new club, he recruited Vincenzo Iaquinta to Turin. Vincenzo was a tall and lean striker from Udinese, who was a lethal weapon against rival defenses, and was worshipped as a god because he worked magic on the pitch.

In his first year on the bench of Juventus, he led the team to place third in the standings. Considerig that he came from Serie B, things had started ideally for Claudio. Everything seemed perfect for the 2007-2008 season. Karma—a word that has always been in Ranieri's vocabulary—indicated that things were ideal and that his goals would be fulfilled. Those were the days, however, when his clashes with Mourinho began. These clashes offered nothing positive to his coaching career.

Juventus did not make a good start and he tacitly resigned from the team. His resignation wasn't accepted by the administration as many still believed in him. Others, however, tripped him up and often misinterpreted things he said.

Any statements or point of view he expressed were distorted, and Claudio realized that he had overstayed his welcome. When during the season he pointed out that Inter was the most powerful rival of Juventus and that they must focus on dealing with that issue, the statement was misinterpreted to mean that Juventus was weak. There were well-wishers who could not forgive such a thing coming from the coach of Juventus. Naturally, he was implying no such thing. It definitely wasn't the reality of the situation. Claudio had merely meant to point out the team's most important opponent. Nothing more, nothing less.

Juventus, which is a big club, and Ranieri, a very experienced coach, were now forced to the ropes of the ring. They were under enormous pressure. He remained with the club, but he knew his days were numbered there. The expiration date of this adventure was soon to come.

An extraordinary meeting of the Board of Juventus Football Club was held and the decision was made to inform the coach of the youth squad, Ciro Ferrara, that he would be coaching Juventus the very next day. Claudio was a thing of the past for Juventus. Needless to say, his stint with Juventus did not end on good terms. In the football world, there was no doubt that Ranieri was a good manager and terrific with public relations, but the fact that his stint with the big clubs had not lead to many achievements made his coaching ability questionable.

He knew his reputation was on the line, but he also knew that there were two things that were not up for negotiation: his dignity and his honesty. It was what distinguished him in all of his partnerships. When things started to go awry, he was the first to step back and make sure to notify those concerned. He did not play crooked PR games or exploit people and secrets he may have known about. He amply showed this with his attitude whenever collaborations ended. Nobody ever accused him of malice. They know what kind of man Ranieri is. Thus whenever a position opened, he was always the first to be considered to fill it.

A life lesson for all of us is to leave with your head held high, even if you know you are being wronged. Believe in your own abilities, and do not be deterred, no matter how difficult things may be. Yes, destiny played some strange games with Claudio, who was well-prepared but fell short of the target many times.

When he was appointed to his beloved Roma's bench in September 2009, no one had even fathomed that by the end of the season they would be just a breath away from winning the Campionato. When Spalletti left Roma, Ranieri took over almost as soon as Spalletti set his foot out the door. It is the team that owned his heart. The team he grew up with. As a child he wore the yellow and red (Giallorossi) jersey, dreaming a thousand dreams of the future. Roma is adored by all its fans. Maybe the team has not won as many titles as other teams, but they enjoy the same level of prestige.

Fans of Roma are loyal and totally identify themselves with the club. They are ambitious and intimately connected to the team. The same applies to the players.

Francesco Totti, a symbol for Roma, did not accept the millions being thrown at his feet from some of the best teams in the world. He spent his entire career wearing his beloved team's jersey, never trading it in for another. His collaboration with Ranieri has been exemplary.

Some coaches have an intense inferiority complex when they are called upon to work with a team that has an emblematic figure in its ranks. They come into conflict with others and eventually they clash. Traditionally, in most cases, these conflicts harm the team first and then the coach. Ranieri rarely argued with the stars of the teams he worked with. He knew that was in no one's best interests. He also respected their personalities.

The Eternal City enjoyed Roma's success for a while under his management. The club's overall performance had improved and the team came close to claiming the championship for the 2009-2010 season. They didn't win, despite the fact that five games before the end they were in the lead. The team even lost the cup to Inter who had previously won the Scudetto.

Everyone was convinced that Ranieri was a loser who would not be able to succeed. He was a good coach who could manage teams well and change the players' psychology for the better, but none of the teams he worked with would ever become champions. His faith and dedication to his goal were unsurpassable. He never lost his courage. Deep down, he knew that some day he would make it. If you lose your faith, you lose everything!

There are talented, fortunate, and very capable people who are able to reach their zenith. Their faith and sacrifice to hit their target generate positive thoughts and positive energy rises from within. The result creates champions. This was Ranieri. A real champion despite not having won a championship. He was already a winner. At the end of the day, in football and in life, you should feel good inside, no matter if you win first place or not.

Claudio felt wonderful inside because he was sure he had put his best foot forward in all that he did. Whenever he talks to anyone, his positive energy is directly conveyed to them. He never gave up and did not curse his bad luck when once again he tried to reach his goal, only to have it to slip through his fingers.

His positive attitude, even in difficult times, sets an example for all. It is his secret weapon. The main thing you notice about him. His personality first, his coaching abilities second. He quickly realized he would not be with his beloved Roma very long. The following year, he was not able to bring the team the desired results.

In February 2011, he resigned after a series of unsuccessful results. The curtain fell without a lot of hoopla.

7

Accountants Worldwide Unite

The five years that followed were a nightmarish experience professionally. The results were not in his favor, but he managed to leave his mark with whatever team he worked with, and he always kept his trademark positive disposition.

From some time before he offered him Inter's bench, Moratti had his eye on Ranieri. He appreciated him greatly, mostly because of his positive attitude and outlook on life. He had been watching him closely for years.

In the summer of 2011, there was a debate concerning Gasperini—the manager of Inter Milan—about whether he could keep the Nerazzurri (black and blues) on top. The uncertainty was quickly justified because Inter was off to a poor start for the 2011-2012 season, facing four defeats out of five matches.

Before Gasperini was politely sent packing, Claudio met Inter's influential president, Massimo Moratti, in Milan. The deal was sealed within ten minutes and Ranieri was to take over Inter Milan.

The collaboration began as with all the teams he worked with in the course of his coaching career. Big wins and impressive performances. The team left the pitch as winners in seven consecutive games. Ranieri was the toast of all Inter's fans. He was being celebrated for another reason as well: in the big derby with AC Milan—in which victory meant a title—Inter won and was back on the championship track.

After that, there were disproportionate expectations, and war sirens began to blare. He was not able to withstand the pressure and the results went downhill. One hundred and eighty-eight days after Moratti hired him and after Inter Milan was defeated by Juventus, he withdrew from the world of Italian football.

It was the end of an era. Claudio would have to plan his next step for the future. At the time, he thought perhaps it would be best to take a step back and give a much needed new impetus to his career.

Lazio and West Bromwich made formal proposals, but the arrival of billionaire Rybolovlev to Monaco is what changed the balance for the days to come. At the end of May 2012, Ranieri was officially appointed coach of Monaco with a two-year contract. It would be his first time on the bench of a French team.

His quest was to reinstate the Monegasque team to the Championnat National, and promote them to first division from second division where they had been previously relegated. He succeeded. The next season, his aim was to do the opposite and usurp Paris Saint-Germain's throne. The eighty points he gathered up with Monaco weren't enough and the principality club parted ways with Ranieri, who earned about 5,000,000 EUR as compensation. Accountants worldwide bent over their calculators and went to work again adding up his assets. They had not yet realized that this story did not harm the Italian, but only slightly bothered those who really knew him. This is due to the fact that much of what we read or hear on a daily basis may not have the slightest grain of truth to it, so we become immune.

I will give my own personal testimony here. We all had our views—which had been cultivated by the media—about Ranieri's agreement with Monaco. After some relevant investigation, the view that had been instilled in my own mind about his compensations changed radically.

In the five times he had been let go of over the last ten years—until the day he was appointed to the national team of Greece—it is said that he earned more than 12,000,000 EUR or about 10,000,000 GBP in compensation from his contracts. When his contract was prematurely terminated with the national team of Greece, the next day all the newspapers wrote about the large compensation he should receive.

It had become fashionable to discuss this issue, thus a pattern had emerged. In times of economic troubles, while the average citizen was suffering, the amounts that were circulating naturally provoked turmoil.

His agreement with the Hellenic Football Federation—the governing body for football in Greece (EPO)—provided for a two-year contract with an annual salary of approximately 800,000 EUR; that is 1,600,000 EUR for two years, with an extra bonus for wins. Agreements in such cases are guaranteed when the name attached to them belongs to someone of high caliber, like Ranieri. When Ranieri agreed to work with the national team of Greece, he was the biggest name to ever be appointed to the team's bench based on his resume and performances in the top clubs throughout Europe.

Prior to the termination of his contract, Ranieri had received an amount which was quite low, just enough so he could pay his associates. During his four-month stay with a two-year contract for 1,600,000 EUR, he had barely received anything. Following his dismissal, everyone wrote about his compensation and his upcoming hard negotiations. As a matter of fact, they wrote that he would not consent to leaving at all if he did not receive the entire amount mentioned in the contract.

Below I have quoted the full text of the commentary which appeared the day after his agreement was terminated with the Hellenic Football Federation. This is what was written:

"Claudio Ranieri takes full responsibility for the performance of the national team in the first four qualifying games of the of the Euro 2016, but he does not seem eager to leave... This creates quite a difficult situation as the cost is enormous.

Furthermore, after the team's last defeat, the Hellenic Football Federation, including the president George Sarris, does not support the Italian tactician's choice to remain. The decision of the EPO to terminate the collaboration with Ranieri is official, but there seems to be a catch in the process since the signed agreement between the EPO and the Italian tactician is quite favorable for him.

The contract does not mention a specific amount to be paid by the EPO as compensation. In order to terminate the agreement with Claudio Ranieri, the EPO must pay the entire amount stated in his contract, up until the last day of its validity. Even with rough calculations, the sum the EPO must pay the Italian tactician exceeds 1,500,000EUR..."

In March 2016, when I arrived at Leicester to prepare an interview for a state-owned television station, I received information from a credible source that about a year and a half after the termination of the agreement with the Hellenic Football Federation, Ranieri agreed to an amount that was light years away from the 1,500,000 EUR.

My source revealed to me that Ranieri hadn't received any money for over a year, except the small deposit that he was obliged to split with his associates. He had yet to receive any money after that. He handed back the second year of his contract to the Federation, but the amount that he and his associates would have received as compensation was never paid.

"It can't be," I thought to myself, "my source must be mistaken. How does a man—who always goes after his compensations, the so-called hard negotiator, the coach who was not the one to prematurely terminate his contract in the first place, and who had not received money either—not tear the EPO to pieces?"

I questioned Ranieri in front of the camera about the compensation issue. I was itching to learn. Some of the EPO agents claimed the Federation had financial problems after Ranieri left as he had collected all his compensation pay. They took it much further and said that there would be no money to offer a good coach to replace Ranieri because they had given all the money to him.

Claudio was very surprised by the question. He did not expect it. At first he gave me a quizzical look as if to say "What is this guy asking me?"

He smiled slightly and looked at the camera knowingly and said, "They are paying me slowly...slowly."

So my source was right! Ranieri had been left unpaid for a year and a half and had not received compensation to boot. Not only that, he was being paid the money he was entitled, but in long-term installments. This is not something new, especially in Greek football. Claudio realized this and had come to terms with it without making waves. He wanted to help the situation, not make it worse. He was honest. Most importantly, he made sure that no great commotion was made about it. He knew that his stint on the bench of the national team had been disastrous, but he was still a professional.

The man who had been made to look like he drove a hard bargain and was a huntsman of payoffs had literally gifted an entire contract year to the EPO, while still waiting for money he should have already been paid.

Well then:

Ranieri's Career in Numbers

Team	Tenure	Wins
Cagliari	1988-1991	31.94%
Napoli	1991-1993	36.00%
Fiorentina	1993-1997	40.00%
Valencia	1997-1999	46.05%
Atletico M.	1999-2000	23.68%
Chelsea	2000-2004	53.77%
Valencia	2004-2005	41.67%
Parma	2007-2007*	43.75%
Juventus	2007-2009	48.94%
Roma	2009-2011	55.56%
Inter	2011-2012	48.57%
Monaco	2012-2014	57.33%

Ranieri's Titles

Team	Title	Year
Fiorentina	Coppa Italia	1996
Valencia	Intertoto Cup	1998
Valencia	Copa del Rey	1999
Valencia	UEFA Super Cup	2004
Monaco	Ligue 2	2013
Leicester	Premier League	2016

8

The Charter Breaks Down En Route to the Mundial

Only a few hours had passed since Hazard scored the goal and the match between Chelsea and Tottenham ended in a draw making Leicester champion, fair and square. Now Claudio Ranieri was to be interviewed on RAI 3, the Italian state-owned station, on the program *Processo del Lunedi* to talk about Leicester's win. But even during that greatest moment of his career, he still felt bitterness about the way things had transpired over the previous months.

His experience on the bench of the Greek national team was traumatic and he had been stigmatized by it. Even though he only appeared to the Greek fans twice—through the interviews we did for the Greek state-owned station—both times he was calm and collected, despite his disappointment. He never meant to spark conflict under any circumstances.

About the match that had just ended and made him champion of England, Ranieri said, "When Hazard scored, I was jumping up and down on the seat." He had been holding onto his hard feelings for some time and found that the right time had come to let it be known.

"I always believed that I could win a title. I remind you that I am the same man who was sacked by Greece about a year and a half ago. Perhaps someone there had forgotten about my career. I am still the same man; I have not changed. The only thing that I can do is to dedicate this victory to those who believed in me."

Generalized bitterness, but also the truth. His four-month stint on the bench of the national team of Greece—with fourteen sessions and four games—was the most devastating partnership of his career, one that in retrospect was equally detrimental to both himself and the Greek national team. The story had begun some time before he arrived on the bench and ended dramatically at the Hotel Vouliagmeni Suites, immediately after the humiliating defeat by Faroe Islands.

Now, the decision to appoint Fernando Santos to the bench of the national team of Greece seemed to have already been taken place long before Greece went to the Mundial of Brazil in 2014. Santos was cleverly presented to the media by press representatives with direct relations to the EPO as someone who desired—long before Greece went to the Mundial—to go back to working with a club every day.

They made it seem as if he had grown tired of the ordeal of the national team and just desired to go back to the daily routine of working with a club. This was only half true because the other half of the truth was that he yearned to remain on the bench of the Greek national team. Various agents of the Hellenic Football Federation—who had a role in things, but no direct connections to the Portuguese tactician—cunningly helped things along by leaking Santos' desire to the press.

The Portuguese coach had his own circle of people he trusted from his previous stint on the benches of Greek teams. He had close ties with the players, presidents, and former presidents of the teams he worked with. He had a trusted inner circle of reporters that he worked with for years, while having created his own team. After seeing that there was no way to connect with the Portuguese coach, but meaning to influence some of his decisions, they tried to create an environment of velvet divorce long before the World Cup games.

The developments that followed, with Santos taking over the national team of Portugal, may have later contradicted those prophecies of doom, but the damage had been done—and right before the Mundial in Brazil.

But of course, what followed was so extreme that it caused many people to forget about the previous events...

The national team of Greece boarded the airplane to fly to Portugal, the USA, and finally Brazil. There was a dark and pensive mood lurking in the atmosphere. The differences that had come about as a result of the recriminations among the teams in the championship were more than self-explanatory. Many times there was great tension in the air due to the intervention of agents who interfered directly with the work of the national team. There were groups of players within the national team who argued almost daily and an ongoing series of similar events did anything but give a preview of the team spirit which was supposed exist for the matches in Brazil.

Fernando Santos seemed trapped when he realized his creation, which had many previous successes—and which he'd so

The Charter Breaks Down En Route to the Mundial

painstakingly built with solidarity and unity as his pillars—was doomed to come crashing down because of the toxic atmosphere.

Shortly before the Mundial of Brazil, Santos expressed the desire to resign. An incident had infuriated him: an agent outside the EPO fancied inviting a particular player to the Mundial. A harsh intervention that the EPO knew of firsthand. The purpose was to increase the player's market value—possible participation in the World Cup—then put him up for sale. The incident turned the coach and the team upside down.

On the way to Brazil, it seemed as though it was every man for himself. The members of the team were not getting along with each other. Various incidents occurred, some made public, some not. Many of them were swept under the rug.

When the team was detained in America and was unable to travel to Brazil, the official announcement stated that the charter plane they would be using had broken down. An urban legend—and the various cliques that formed during that time—spoke of the lack of organization on the part of the EPO and also the fact that the team was not properly prepared for the Mundial. A scenario circulating in America was that the deal fell through for the charter's rent, because no official deal even existed before the team left Greece. When the team arrived in New York, the owners of the charter asked for more money to take them to Brazil.

I am not sure if this is true, but given the way the national team finally arrived to play at the Mundial, it is highly likely this did occur. Someone thought up the story about the charter malfunction and the team being unable to leave the USA. Even if this were true, if the charter had really broken down, and if everything else was just rumors, the EPO was still responsible, as was their representative who was put in charge of organizing the trip.

The agreement the EPO had with the airline should have ensured the trip well in advance, especially since the country's national team was traveling to play in the Mundial. In case anything should happen to prevent the flight, by any fault of the airline, arrangements should have been made for the team to be transported, no matter what. The team was not on the way to a scrimmage match. Of course, this had not been foreseen in the contract, as it turned out. Everything was haphazardly planned, resulting in the players and Santos being stranded in America, looking for a way to get to Brazil.

Half of the mission requested to return to Greece and travel to Brazil from Athens on the eve of the opening game. This would have been disastrous for the team and all their preparation would have gone down the drain. Santos adamantly refused and was looking for a way to get his team to the Mundial before the games commenced by himself.

Accompanied by only one agent of the Federation, who spoke no English, communication for arrangements was non-existent. The players took the initiative and personally made phone calls to find an airplane to finally get to Brazil. At dawn, the president of a team who owned airplanes was called to try to find a solution. The image of the lot of them standing around the hotel lobby in America trying to find alternatives for the team to travel was an upsetting and pitiful sight. All this just a few days prior to the first game.

The chosen solution was to travel with a commercial airline, but even in this case, it still was a lot of trouble because there were

The Charter Breaks Down En Route to the Mundial

not enough tickets to cover group seating since they had been forced to get the tickets at the last minute. But there was no other way, so they started out for Brazil with part of the team sitting in business class, some in economy with the passengers. Tragicomedy in all its glory, starring a team that had been the European champion some ten years ago.

Some of the members of the medical team, physiotherapists, and assistants were almost bumped from the flight because there was a waiting list.

Along with the prevailing disorganization, the poisonous atmosphere which was still maintained by some even during the matches overshadowed the good performance the team had in the Mundial.

The moral of this story is: if for various reasons the players of a team or members of the crew operate professionally on an individual level, as soon as they all come together, miracles can happen.

The national team of Greece's participation in the Mundial of Brazil was indeed another miracle, which almost did not happen because of the fiasco that took place before.

9

Kings in England and Europe: Driven Away From Greece

All the previously mentioned events took place before the appointment of Ranieri to the national team of Greece. The fact that Santos left Brazil to go to his home country instead of returning to Greece with his team was a telltale sign that the problem was profound and irreversible. In Greek football, the shots are called by those who have special interests.

Ranieri was entering into unknown territory on a wing and prayer, and his trusted colleagues never informed him of the essential details. Santos was not allowed to return with his team in order to thank the people. Claudio Ranieri had no idea what the agents were doing.

I traveled to Estoril, two months after the Mundial, to meet with Fernando Santos so he could give a statement for the first time since the Brazilian adventure. He was greatly saddened he had not been allowed to return to Greece with his lads, his players.

Our interview caused quite a sensation for the Greek press and it became headline news. Santos opened his heart to the Greek fans after the very good performance in the Mundial of Brazil.

Kings in England and Europe: Driven Away From Greece

"Everyone knows what your country means to me. This love flourished in 2001 when I came to Greece for the first time. I have a special love for Greece that will never change. It will not change now that I am the manager for the national team of Portugal. I am Portuguese and I am happy to be here in my country. But the years I was working with the teams in Greece, I felt Greek."

With his emotions written all over his face, he continued, "Greece is my second home and I will always have you all in my heart. I think about the Greek people every day. I think about the economic crisis the people are going through. I will never forget about Greece. I am certain that I will return many times. I do not know if it will be for work in the future. Nobody knows. I will come to see my friends and the country that I love so very much. The four years I was with the national team were very important to me, I worked with great players. We had a special bond with all of the players from all the teams. This bond exists still today and I want it to be like this for many years to come. I have lifetime friends that I will always keep in my heart.

"I always want Greece to win, no matter where the team is playing. Things are different here; there is another ambience. It is not right to separate my players; I do not like to do that. I cannot only speak of Ronaldo or the other great players I have worked with. I want to discuss tactics and technique when I talk about my teams. The most important thing for me is that we all progressed quite well when I was with the Greek team. I am happy because now is a powerful moment for me. I am the coach for Portugal, and that is a big deal. I cannot hide the fact that I felt the same way when I started to work in Greece. When I said yes to the proposal, I felt honored they were giving me the chance to work with the national team of Greece. I cannot compare the teams of Greece and Portugal, nor the players, it is not right, I have never done it. I worked hard all these years. We fought very hard to make it with the Greek team and I am proud of us for all we accomplished."

At that point, wanting to prompt him to speak about the issue that all of Greece was talking about—that many agents of the EPO were holding him personally responsible—I asked him straight out why he did not return to Greece with the team.

"They wrote many different things about why I did not return to Greece. Some of the people from the team did not properly explain what happened. I do not want to say too much on the matter, but people should know that what transpired after the Mundial was not my responsibility. I did what I was told to do and acted upon what was organized. I had airplane tickets that I did not make reservations for myself and traveled by plane with the tickets that were purchased by the Hellas Football Federation. I would like you to know I have great respect for the Greek people. I respect my colleagues. I bid farewell to one of my players and it was very emotional. But I have something pending and I want you to know that I want to return to Greece as soon as possible; I really want to thank everyone from the bottom of my heart. I was not able to express my gratitude, so I would like to return to Greece for that. Those who know me personally know very well that I will never change. My heart will always be in your country. I did not watch the match between Greece and Romania, but when I learned of Greece's defeat, I was upset. I expected Greece to win that match, but many times people think some matches will be easy, but no matches are easy. I am not at all pleased that Greece lost, because I love the national team. When Greece plays at the same time as Portugal, I am sure you will understand that I cannot be present to watch the Greek team play. I often think about the team and I believe people are happy with the team, so they should stand behind it."

He had already revealed how the national team operated. A few days before our interview in Estoril with Fernando Santos, Ranieri's debut had begun to seem challenging. There were some occurrences that proved it would be best if someone were to stand with the Italian and act as a barrier to block the waves of any arising issues.

Giorgos Karagounis is an emblematic figure in the history of Greek football. He has worn his jersey more times than any other player. His appointment was unhindered and, through summary proceedings, he had been given the role of technical director. This made an impression on Santos:

"I would like for Karagounis to enjoy the same successful career in the Federation as he had as a player. As a player, he was incredible and a role model for all, not only for his talent, but for the passion he has on the pitch. Those who are on the national team should live by Karagounis' example.

"I want Kara to be happy and to help the national team. I do not want him to change. I wish for Greece to continue doing well and to play in France in 2016. I will not hide the fact that my greatest dream is to see Portugal and Greece together. Katsouranis could have remained on the high level he was, but he wanted to go to another championship; he made history as well, just like Zagorakis, Tsartas, and Delias did in the past. In the Mundial, both Karagounis and Katsouranis and the other lads wrote their own history because for the first time we were qualifiers.

"Many players made history in Greek football, but the last few years they were the ones who were able to upgrade the team, and they did just that. I believe that Katsouranis will excel very much in his career, and I hope he does. Why not the Greek championship? I believe that in January he can return and play on a high level again. It is very difficult for me to talk about the people. It is not easy for me. I would like to express my deepest gratitude. The fact remains that Santos has not changed and he will never change. Everybody knows that one of the reasons that I left was because I did not agree with the financial terms. The EPO made a new proposal, I did not agree with it. When one of the two parties refuses, collaboration cannot continue. It was the same when I with PAOK and I said yes to the Hellenic Football Foundation. It was not easy for any coach to take Rehhagel's place then, but when I agreed, I had followed my heart. Just like when I was coaching the Greek national team, I always followed my heart for everything. After the four years, for me, many circumstances had changed. There were other important things afterwards that changed as well; it was not my heart, which was always Greek. We had to agree on other things for the new contract. We did not agree but that does not mean that my love changed for Greece or for the Greek people."

Destiny plays some strange games...

Fernando Santos—twenty months and a few days after our interview in Estoril—wrote the story of the European championship in golden letters.

Claudio Ranieri—seventeen months after leaving the national team of Greece—led Leicester to victory in England.

Kings in England and Europe: Driven Away From Greece

They were both kings in England and Europe, but driven away from Greece. Coincidence? Maybe. The harsh reality is that in Greek football positivity never thrives.

Fernando Santos, with Cristiano and his lads, became European champions in 2016, on the pitches of France, leaving the entire world speechless because Portugal was considered an outsider from the beginning of the tournament.

Ranieri won the title with a bunch of unknown players, and in Greece lack of faith continues to reign.

10

Excuse Me, Sirs...Who Is the President?

Claudio Ranieri, not being aware of all the conditions that existed before he boarded the plane to come and work with the national team of Greece, was forced to work around two points. The first point was that he was requested to build a team, which would not only play for a good result, but would also offer entertainment to the spectators. The second point was to pump positive energy back to the national team of Greece, so the negative frame of mind would be a thing of the past.

Something he did not know, however, was to what extent the mood had deteriorated, because he had not been informed about the negative climate among the members of the team. He was told about the team's performance in Brazil, and generally was informed of what everyone had already seen on television, but was told nothing of the behind-the-scene issues. This meant that since Claudio was ignorant about the negative climate, he did not know he needed to deal with that from the beginning, so he focused mainly on training.

His manager certainly bears a great responsibility who, at times, was criticized for his work with the national team. The most fatal mistake was not informing Ranieri about the issues the team was having, obviously intending to convince him to take over the team as soon as possible. He just wanted to be done with it.

The thought process of the EPO—and the general desire of those who were involved with the Greek team after they returned from Brazil—was to bring in a coach from central Europe to take over; the first option was M.G., a coach who had been managing an English club, had good knowledge of Greek football, and knew a lot of people. He had also once helped a player transfer take place, so they had an obligation towards him because the amounts involved had caused quite a stir.

The second option was M.M., but they were more in favor of M.G. The media and the press mostly talked about M.M. since his personality was closer to that of the Greeks. He was demanding with the players, tough with discipline, and always ready to fight the wrath of gods and demons. Only a small minority of agents believed that, due to many instances where lack of discipline reigned on the Greek team, M.M. would be the perfect candidate to take over. Of course, the agents' opinion did not really matter.

G.S. had taken on the role of negotiator in the discussions for a new coach, due to the fact that he spoke five foreign languages and would therefore be able to communicate with Ranieri.

G.S. contacted M.M., and his wife, who speaks Spanish, was the interpreter. During consecutive telephone conversations, M.M. would request different things each time, ranging from a large staff to a new training center, and a contract much greater than what Santos had.

The negotiations did not go on for long before they eventually fell through. That was when Ranieri emerged as an option. The meeting with Ranieri was to take place in Rome with agents who went on behalf of the Hellenic Football Federation. Ranieri had his associates with him. It was to everyone's advantage that some of the people in the group spoke Italian, so Claudio was informed firsthand, and was able to speak freely.

The discussions went wonderfully and the group got along very well. The only problem was caused by someone in the group, who was seemingly nervous and on his mobile phone every five minutes. He would rise from the table, step away, and when he would return he would put a different issue on the table, with the obvious intention of spoiling the deal. He asked what everyone was saying because he did not know Italian. He was anxious to inform someone about how the meeting was progressing. It was a humorous sight and Claudio had a smile on his face.

At some point he must have asked himself: Who is the one in charge here? Who is the president? It was a bit of an awkward climate. But in the end, they all left the table of one mind, except for one: the person who was on his mobile throughout the meeting. His mission turned into a fiasco since he was not able to pass on the messages to his superior correctly. Ranieri was in agreement with everything and decided to become the coach of the national team of Greece. From day one, things gradually declined for Claudio.

On October 28, 2014, when I arrived in Rome to meet Ranieri for the first and only exclusive interview he gave for the state-owned television station as coach of the Greek national team, the mood was miserable due to the team's constant negative results in the qualifying rounds of the European championship. The way the events were conveyed to the public attributed the responsibility to Ranieri who quite often turned a blind eye.

Even though he was the most famous manager to ever take over the Greek national team, he was never promoted enough. Agents of the EPO are greatly responsible for this because they never managed to buff up the name of the new coach. Instead, they bogged the Italian tactician down with internal political rivalries, not giving him space to maneuver properly. Ranieri's mistake was that he did not establish boundaries from the very first minute. He trusted the people close to him, but most of them acted in their own best interests, and not in his.

Although it did not take long for him to become aware of what was happening and begin distancing himself, it was too late to try and change the situation. He was given incorrect information about various players, such as Katsouranis and Gekkas. They told him that some of the players would be leaving so he need not take them into consideration, excluding them from the list of potential players. They even went so far as to mention straight out that Katsouranis should not be called to the Greek national team ever again because he had a bad reputation and would destroy the team.

So one of the two captains—the one who had been playing the longest, who had been a shield against dozens of problems in the past, and at times had to deal with the team himself—had suddenly acquired a bad reputation and should not be playing in the national team of Greece.

He was given misleading information about other players as well. They stressed that these players were talented and important, and had the potential to excel so he would consider them for the team, thus increasing their market value. They also assigned him associates, who were strangers to him. Some spoke for him publicly, people he had never even said good morning to. There were many rumors circulating that were not even close to reality.

All this was because G.S. came to an agreement with Ranieri instead of M.G., the preferred choice of people inside and outside of the Hellenic Football Federation. They managed to ruin anything having to do with his work with the national team of Greece from the beginning, basically placing a headstone over his presence on the team's bench.

Ranieri failed because from the start the system immediately brushed him aside. The games were continuous and he seemed doomed because even his close associates and the man who had brought him to Greece could not explain to him the true nature of things.

His thoughts on the Greek players were expressed in an interview he gave to me for NERTT (a state-owned broadcaster), just a few days before he left, and they were still positive. He believed in talent, but in teamwork as well, something he attempted to reinstate but was not successful in doing with the Greek national team. His confusion came from being promised things totally different from what really came to be. The players did not acknowledge him and spoke negatively about him in public.

Our interview was a hit and published in virtually every publication and online newspaper. There were people from the EPO who spread various inaccuracies before the interview was publicized; they could not believe that Ranieri was exposing

Excuse Me, Sirs...Who Is the President?

them by choosing to open his heart and reach out to his Greek supporters himself.

The untruths that were spread about him—that were not denied by the people of the EPO, who many times allowed the rumors to circulate with their blessing—had been heard and were well-known. He was considered responsible for all the plights of the national team and of course for their results. It was a standard tactic of those who for many years can earn massive salaries by finding someone to blame. In any given situation, someone else was to blame, but never the agents of the EPO themselves, who set the framework to begin with. Some were even facing accusations for various offences during their stay in the Federation.

There was no room for excuses when it came to the team's results and that is because indeed Ranieri was responsible for the most part. He took on things he knew nothing about and paid dearly for them afterwards.

There were those who tried to stop our interview from being broadcast with tall tales of the subtitled translations being inaccurate and who took it upon themselves to exaggerate the truth about the best coach that had ever worked in the Greek football sector.

11

Bombs Falling Everywhere

Claudio was searching for ways to communicate with the Greek supporters, but the EPO had never given him the opportunity. I was officially approached by his associate who requested to meet with me.

I was initially very skeptical about what he wanted to discuss with me. I too had criticized Ranieri rather strongly. Any commentary I had made, however, was always above the belt without any malice whatsoever. All of us were naive to the fact that there was rampant misinformation spread by several centers of power within the EPO. Their goal was obvious; they wanted to strike a blow at his image so that they could put the blame on him for the defeat.

My meeting with Ranieri's representative was at a hotel. I was with one of my collaborators, who was watching discretely from a distance, just in case his intervention was needed should any mishaps occur.

I had criticized Ranieri and the system, and now they were asking to meet with me; I had to at least cover my back. Journalism has become a rather difficult profession in Greece, and those that are powerful within the football system can sometimes be ruthless.

Many journalists have been badly beaten, while threats are a daily occurrence. The conditions are dreadful, as are the protection systems for the professionals. Without reason, one can suddenly find oneself in an unfortunate situation.

All of my fears were soon dispelled, however, because Ranieri's representative was a gracious young man, who was studying in Italy. Claudio had covertly hired him to monitor what was happening in Greece and to inform him about how the media was dealing with matters that involved him. He realized that he was not being given the truth and was instead being misled in order to be disgraced. So he hired someone local to retrieve information. At least this is what the young man told me when he introduced himself to me. The move of hiring the student should have been made the first day he came to Greece.

He told me that Claudio appreciated the fact that that I mostly critiqued the matches or the tactics he used. I never stepped over the line when commenting, even when everyone else was against him. He was grateful for this, so he was inviting me into his home. I politely requested that I be the one to choose the day of our interview because I wanted to catch the rest of the system off guard.

If it leaked that Claudio was going to give me an interview before it even took place, they would do anything in their power to bring it to a grinding halt. I chose the morning of October 28, 2014—a national holiday in Greece—and boarded the first airplane of the day to fly to Rome.

Claudio greeted us at his three-story home in Lucca Parioli. He opened the door wide. He was very hospitable. The crew and I were there for five hours. Ranieri spoke to us about everything that had transpired. He felt troubled by it all. He had been on the bench of the Greek national team for only three matches but had seen everything: indifferent players, agents coming and going into the changing rooms, wheeler-dealers literally playing on his intelligence, disappointing results with unequal opponents...

I was already aware that it was not suitable for him. The players were not cooperative and would not follow his tactics. Some of them even went to the president of the EPO asking that Ranieri be removed. One of them, without an inkling of discretion or shame, rang Claudio up and asked him for an invitation to Leicester. Ranieri obliged him willingly. He held no grudges because he felt he was mostly to blame for putting himself through such tribulations; he should have known better having experienced so many things in his coaching career.

He requested that I ask him about everything. He did not want to leave anything out. He wanted the fans to learn the truth from him. Claudio began our interview by explaining the idea behind his becoming coach for the national team of Greece.

"I have been in Greece many times. I love the Greek people and after meeting the Greek football players, and seeing them on the pitch in Europe, I said that coaching the national team would be a new job that I would like to do. I wanted to face a new challenge, which is why I accepted the proposal. I met with Yiannis Bethanis and Sarris in Rome. They wanted to meet me before the team left for the Mundial. They wanted to speak with some coaches to see who is available. After we met in Rome, that's where it all began..."

The national team's back was up against the wall at that time. They were off to a rough start in the qualifying matches for the European championship of 2016, which would take place in France.

"I honestly did not expect such a start from the team. I knew it would be difficult. When your coach is replaced, it can be stressful to have a new coach. The players do not know me and I do not know them 100%, so they don't know exactly what I am asking them to do. When returning from a tournament such as the Mundial, many teams sometimes suffer a decline, because all their energy has been exhausted. We saw Holland and Portugal, and Germany having a difficult time bouncing back from their post-Mundial condition, but I also think that some players don't play anymore and some are injured. Another thing that plays a role is if there is a lack of determination and focus. All of these things are factors which made us lose the last two competitions, and for our match to end in a draw with Finland."

Claudio knew that everyone expected for him to bring results and he was looking for a way to do that:

"The best thing we need to keep in our minds is that because we cannot want everything all at once, in order to make a change, time is needed. Constant training is needed. It is one thing to train a team every day for a longer period of time, the coach's philosophy will eventually pass to the player's DNA, and it is another thing to train for only three or four days before a match, especially when the players are already under pressure because of the different problems their team is facing."

He knew it was imperative for changes to be made:

"Someone will be tired, someone might be slightly injured and not 100% ready to train the next day. All this will result in less time, which is needed for the players to absorb the philosophy of the new coach. During my career, my main principle is to fight on the pitch, to give everything for the jersey I wear, for the fans, for the team. This is why I want my players to give everything on the pitch, the maximum of their capabilities. We must be strong and have spirit. When I see that you cannot give me this, I will give you another chance, I will even give you two chances, but after that, I must change something."

After the Mundial, when he took over the national team of Greece and was calling in players, the general impression was that he didn't know the players and that they were being pointed out to him by his associates:

"Right now we have lost many important members of the team, players with vigor, with character, that is the core of it all. We are trying to rebuild the team. The players must have these qualities on the field. Because the coach will have the character, but it is the players who go onto the pitch and must give everything for the national team. This is why I prefer the newer players, even if they do not have much experience. But they must give everything on the pitch."

Ranieri had his own aspirations for the national team of Greece since after his long career, he wanted to attempt something new, but also to succeed on the bench of a national team.

"Now I understand the Greeks are asking to see their national team attack. Yes, it is the right thing to attack, to always be attacking, but we must always be careful of the counterattacks as well. Like with Ireland, they scored because we were hit with counterattacks, and that is not good. We must all be very careful. We should all participate, and I should be smart enough to know that all these years the national team had wins always in the 1-0, 2-1 range, so we should give everything and have a win from a free kick. But you have to have the players who are able to play aggressively. I also like the players who can score one, two, three goals, but there must be a striker that knows how to score. We have to connect the old philosophy with the new philosophy. It takes time to accomplish this."

He could not prejudge the future at that time, but when speaking to him you understand that it did not seem particularly bleak to him:

"Now we have to go match by match. For us every game must be played like it's a final. Our next match is with Faroe Islands and we must play only to win. It will not be easy because they all play defense and will try to counterattack. We must be smart and fast. We must seriously want to win. I want to see my players eat the grass, to be cunning; I want for us to do everything to win the match. We must take it match by match; we must not make any mistakes. When the national team is with their back against the wall, they always find solutions, they always play better. I want to give the players the message that this will be the game of their lives. They must give the maximum of their capabilities so that we can win."

He was never truly satisfied working with the national team of Greece, but he knew that he had to keep the balance.

"The thought of giving up never crossed my mind. I am a man with an agenda and I want the maximum from myself. I ask the same of my players."

He knew the players of the national team, and he also knew their capabilities, which he could help with.

"Winning is everything, but to play aggressive football, champions are needed, the very best players are needed. You want your players to know how to dribble past their opponent, like Cristiano Ronaldo does. Without players who have that ability, you cannot play aggressive football. You want a player who will excite the crowd. He is one of a kind and we do not have players like that. If my players are champions of this type, then they must prove it, because it is different to play offence or to do what the previous national team did for so long. I always face the dilemma whether we should play offence or if we should play to win with a one-goal difference.

"We have seen that by playing in a certain way, our opponents respect us very much because the teams we play in the UEFA league are lower than us. They respect us, but they also know what to expect. They play the way Greece always did. This is an issue that the national team is facing and we must be careful with our defense, not like with Ireland who scored against us with a corner kick.

"The issue is not if we play defensive or aggressive football. It was a set-up play that we should have been careful of and the lads should know they will need to play more aggressively as well. I should explain to them that, yes, we play aggressively, but we need to be sharp and cunning."

Claudio loved Greece long before he came to the bench of the national team:

"I always say that we are close to the Greeks. All of us in the Mediterranean are alike. I came to Greece for the first time when I was a football player with Roma. We played a friendly match, and from that moment on I was captivated. My children studied Greek history, they read Elytis and Homer. We are generally fascinated with Greece. We would always come to Greece for vacations, to the amazing islands, with the beautiful people, who are very open-hearted, and hospitable. I always chose Greece over other countries. When the president called me, I gladly accepted, and I was very happy to come to Greece.

"I was a player for many years on Southern Italian teams—Catania, Catanzaro, Palermo—and I see the same love and passion as the south Italians had with the Greeks now. I feel as though I am at home when I come to Athens or other parts of Greece. I have played for many years in south Italy, so I know exactly how the people are feeling when they go to work the day after their team has won. All of their problems are set aside for a while and they are looking at everything with more positivity.

"Football is very important to the fans for their psychology as well. I know this very well, and I want the players to know and feel it too. The players do understand—and should understand—how much good or harm they do their fans that come to the matches. It is difficult, because I had the good fortune to have a lot of champion players. You mentioned Zola before, who was a player that could define a whole team. Zola was a player who made difficult things seem easy. I had many experiences in my career, but I have one that I distinguish from the rest. My experience in

Cagliari. I was not an excellent football player, I was a normal player of Serie A, on a team that fluctuated, but we always were fighting for the goal. That happened with Catanzaro as well; we were in second division for three years. We won two and lost the one year in the playoffs, and then in Catania, so we stayed in Serie A for five years. The same thing with Palermo. We fought very hard. I was never the best football player and I started from very a low level. I started going step by step and reached the point where I was working with the biggest clubs of Europe. I am still galloping inside, like in Cagliari, where from third division we galloped to the second and from the second to the first division. All this within three years. This was my takeoff point. During my career and all my life, I remember that team and the fans.

"I feel pressured a lot because I am the first person to put myself under pressure. I always want the maximum from myself and from the players. But I know well that we are not giving 100%. I will take all the pressure upon myself because I am a positive person and I am used to being under pressure. I want to generate positive energy from this pressure. I hope that the players, who surely feel the pressure as well, will also generate positive energy into the match with Faroe Islands."

At that point, he sent his own message to the Greek people.

"The thing I don't like is the results because the Greek people are not happy. After the Mundial, people are expecting something good, something positive, and we have not given this to them. My frustration is because we are not giving the Greek people what they deserve. In order for us to give more, we must work with the lads more, because we are slowly changing from one style of playing to another. We cannot have everything at once. We are falling behind because I cannot be with them every day. I have to ask for the maximum of the players' capabilities within just four days. Then I see them one month later and then after four months, it is a challenge.

"I understand, and I knew from the start, and now I realize it even more. I am disappointed that I cannot show my character to the lads who are going to the pitch, and that is what frustrates me even more."

About the support of his Greek fans:

"I realize we have not been able to give the Greek fans what they wanted, but I ask them to support us at this time because it is very important for the lads to feel as if they are playing at home."

His request to the EPO for the younger generation:

"A few months ago, the Federation had requested me to see what we can do for the younger generation. Because I could not train the youth team, I suggested to the EPO to speak with Christian Damiano. He was my assistant coach for Juventus, Roma, Inter, and Parma. He was a coach at Clairefontaine. For those who do not know, Clairefontaine is the elite national center that trains new football players. Various players were produced from Clairefontaine, such as Trezeguet, Thierry Henry, Gallas, and many others. When I was in St. Petersburg recently, Germany's coach, the winner of the world cup, was asked a question.

"They asked him, 'How did you come to winning the Mundial?' He told them the story from the beginning. When Klinsmann came to the national team, the first thing he asked for was to establish an academy for the younger generation of football players. That is where the newer generation came from. I mentioned this to the EPO, that we need a person in charge of the academy for the younger players, a person who would be able to choose the coaches, because the younger generation is our future. Greece has many young players, but they are not trained. We need to establish a football academy.

"We should look in different areas with the coaches and find the best players. To find the most capable players, not someone's friend. It is very wrong to make someone a football player who is not good enough. We have to think on a higher level. To bring young football players, who have no sponsors to help them, but deserve to play professional football. The future of Greece, Italy, and of all countries is the new generation. You have to find the right people to take these lads to the top."

At that time he had been accused about the choices of coaches for the smaller national teams. The names chosen even caused uproar and an issue arose of whether or not Ranieri had even decided on them himself:

"Please hold me responsible only for what I have actually done myself. I do not know anyone, and since I do not know anyone from the smaller national teams, how could I put someone there? Hold me responsible for the first team, the national men's team, not for the smaller national teams. You can hold me responsible for the smaller national teams if EPO hires Christian Damiano, then I will be responsible, but not this time."

His relationship with Karagounis remained perfect even after he left the national team of Greece. Above all, it was a down-to-earth relationship and very sincere. Claudio had invited Karagounis to the match between Leicester and Newcastle at King Power. Giorgos Karagounis is an especially well-known player outside of Greece. Shortly before the match, he walked through the entrance of the VIP section, and once the Leicester fans took notice of him, they were very excited and crowded around him asking for his autograph and to take pictures with him. He wrote his own history in Greek football. In the interview, Ranieri told us:

"Since I'm not able to train the team all the time, I needed someone who knows everything in detail. I needed someone who knows the psychology and differences between the players in Greece. When I heard that Giorgios was free—and I know he is a serious person, a man who will look straight into your eyes and will never betray you—I asked him if he could come and be part of our staff. He is someone who knows all of the national team. He has been part of this team for twenty years.

"We have an excellent relationship and we discuss everything, about players, about the qualities of the players. I asked him to speak to the players abroad, to the injured players, and then to inform me. I exchange many views with Karagounis."

12

Left in the Dark

Claudio came to the meeting tanned from days of swimming in the sea. After the contract signing, the president of the EPO, George Sarris, a doctor from the island of Chios, wanted their official photo taken in front of the Portugal EURO replica trophy.

The atmosphere was pleasant and, in this first meeting, Ranieri was willing to talk about many things, but a major press conference would be taking place a few days later in a hotel in the center of Athens.

It was a two-part contract for two-plus-two years with the national team of Greece, which would be extended only after reaching the target, when the team qualified for the final in the European Championship of France in 2016.

The extension option was a formality, because during those summer days nobody believed what would occur in the following months.

He was the best coach to ever come to the bench of the national team of Greece. He arrived at a time when, for the last five years, his career had been at a stand-still. No other club had shown much interest because none of his teams really had any great achievements. His decision to work with a national team surprised those who follow football closely.

He knew very well that he was on new territory, but the national team of Greece's performance only days before the Mundial—and the opponents they were to play against—gave him a lot of work to do. He wanted to have some idea about the players, so it was suggested that he travel to Brazil to see the team play before the announcement was made about his appointment to the team.

The Greek football scene was eventful at the time due to inter-team rivalries. Claudio's logical approach did not allow the agents' wishes for him to go to Brazil to be fulfilled. He did not even discuss it. He was very experienced and knew that it would have a negative impact on him and the team if he were to sit in the stands to watch the games. The progress was excellent, but he did not have as real a picture as he would have had he seen the team play live on the pitch.

The EPO estimated that if the national team qualified for EURO France in 2016, the option of extension for another two years would be purely a formality on Ranieri's contract. He wanted to work, and was very willing to do so, which is proven by the fact that he asked for the extension option to be included in the contract himself. The agreement provided that Ranieri would receive 800,000 EUR for each contract year. He would receive a bonus of an extra 800,000 EUR if the national team of Greece completed the qualifying rounds of the European championship undefeated. But the team had to win every qualifying match, otherwise he would not get the bonus, regardless of whether the team won the championship or not. The team must be undefeated in the qualifying phase.

He was totally satisfied with the agreement and in his first public statements he praised the president of the EPO for helping him to arrive to the decision to come to work in Greece.

"Although I also had some other proposals, as soon as I met with the president, I got a good feeling. I already knew the Greek national team well, so I agreed. I thought it would be a good move to continue my career in Greece."

He knew how the team played in the Mundial, but he had only seen what everyone else had seen. At the time he had not been informed in detail. In a way, it was only logical that he had not bonded with the team.

"I saw how Greece played at the Mundial. They made good progress and I loved their spirit. We want to continue this but also the hard work. We will aim to produce the best results in the Euro 2016."

Ranieri had said that he would be keeping the core of the national team of Greece, but something else came to light instead:

"There should not be many changes to the core of the team, but we will know more as we progress, when all the players can be evaluated."

Enough had been revealed to know where this was all leading, from his first day, when he was asked what he would be doing about Santos' associates. In previous years, they had done a very good job on all levels. The question was if some of the members would be remaining: "Up until now, there have been no such discussions, and I have my own associates with me."

Later, when things with the EPO began to falter, he revealed that he had not met anyone from Santos' team, but not because he did not want to. When Santos worked in Greece, he had applied his own system, which had been successful. His staff would bring him information weekly from a database about the players that were on other teams and were able to be called in.

Everyone was put under a microscope, ready to be called in at any given moment. The details of each player's condition were known firsthand, not only of the men's national team, but also of the smaller national teams.

Santos' assistant, Leonidas Vokolos, with the technical director but also with the members of the medical team, would load all the relative information into the database. The crew had exceptional members, like Christos Karvounidis, a physiotherapist, who is otherwise known as Magic Hands. A few months later he was also shown the exit door from the national team.

When Ranieri took over, no one bothered to give him any information, not even the standard procedure of receiving and delivery of the information about players, which was an asset of the EPO. They never brought him into contact with Santos or with any of his associates, so that he could be directly informed and get the information to make his own assessments. He had been left completely in the dark.

The result was catastrophic for everyone. At that time, the agents in the EPO wanted, in any way possible, to be rid of anything that reminded them of the situation that existed in the past with the team, because apart from the previous coach, many players were unwanted by the system.

When they gave him the list with the names of the players who were available to be called to the national team, there were more than thirty names. But Ranieri was troubled because some of the most fantastic players that had earlier taken the national team to the second round of the World Cup were missing. He did not have the time, though, to discover exactly what occurred within each case, because the qualifying phase for the EURO of France had begun.

13

Unsuccessful Attempts

Matt Scott is a columnist for the website insideworld-football.com. When Ranieri left the Greek national team, Scott posted a rather harsh article about the reasons behind the Italian manager's failure.

The article mentions the rather bad state of Greek football over the last several years and mainly touches upon the corruption within the system. The article extensively describes Ranieri's declining managerial reputation in Greece:

"In Greek mythology Dionysus, or Bacchus, was an unborn child when his pregnant mother was killed and he was rescued by his father, Zeus, later to be born from the thigh of the god. Dionysus became the Greek god of the harvest, the symbol of death and resurrection.

"As Leicester City fans indulge in much-merited bacchanalias in tribute to their unlikely triumph in this season's Premier League campaign, it is the powerful, smiling lion, Claudio Ranieri, who has been reborn.

"Ranieri took the job at Leicester less than two years after being dismissed as coach of the Greek national team in what was for him the nadir of his 30-year career as a football manager. His record in his short time with Greece was appalling, to be frank. They had entered Euro 2016 qualifying as the seventh-ranked team in Europe and were top in their group. The campaign began at home with a 1-0 defeat by Romania, followed by a 1-1 draw in Finland. Then Northern Ireland beat Greece 2-0 in Athens, followed by Ranieri's final ignominy, a 1-0 defeat at home to the Faroe Islands, the latter's first competitive away victory in 13 years. He was promptly sacked. How could it be that a man so chastened by what happened as manager of Greece could now be feted as King Claudio, as he was on Monday's *Gazzetta dello Sport* front page? How could he be crowned champion of England after winning the Premier League title with Leicester City?

"The story of Leicester City's success has been well documented and it is not for me to rehearse it here. What is of more value is an exploration of the circumstances Ranieri faced as manager of the Greek national team. The first thing to note is that the Italian was not alone in failing to rouse Greece to the standards expected of them.

"A little more than ten years after winning the Euro 2004 tournament, Greece contrived to finish bottom of their qualifying group with only one win from 10 matches, six of them under another manager. Not that the task should have been too tricky. With Hungary making up the numbers, Greece's qualifying opponents were teams who in the 56-year history of the European Championships had qualified for only six tournaments between them, four of them Romania's and the other two Hungary's, from 1964 and 1972. Their average ranking was 33 among the 54-team UEFA list. In short, Greece was not facing titans of the international game yet still they sunk like a sailor who has angered Poseidon. The Faroes did the double over them. So what was it down to? If a national team is the expression of its domestic league, then the atrophy of Greece's performance in an international competition is undoubtedly a symptom of the lack of competition in the Super League."

Claudio knew how to court the media and used it to the best of his ability, whenever he wanted the spotlight turned on him. In a statement to the newspaper *Corriere*, he said that he regretted becoming the manager of the national team of Greece even before the downfall.

14

Greece Was My Mistake

"Skepticism is a part of the football world that judges you superficially.

"I made a mistake to accept Greece's proposal; I was only able to train 14 days, and had only 4 games. I was sacked after we were defeated by the Faroe Islands. In Leicester, I proved that I am not a loser."

That is what he said about the Greek national team, a chapter that he had since closed and put behind him.

After he left the Greek bench, most people put Claudio Ranieri under fire. This could be considered a completely natural reaction, if one takes into consideration the way in which Greece was disqualified, but also because of the humiliation the fans felt from the defeat. Claudio took the responsibility and most of the share of the blame for the performance of Greece. He could not do anything else. His career had been severely damaged. No one went to the airport to see him off. He said nothing, he just gathered up his belongings and left. He arrived a gentleman and four months later, he walked away a gentleman.

Many wrote about Ranieri's failure, even after Leicester won the title. Some seized the opportunity to make their own analysis. In the land of democracy, everyone has the right to express their opinion, of course, even if it is obvious they don't have the slightest idea about football. Everyone was fighting for a small piece of the publicity they might gain through his name.

Various people spoke publicly about Ranieri, but one that made a lasting impression was a member of the Greek Parliament, who after Leicester's title win posted a highly nauseating post on his Facebook page.

Everyone's opinion should be respected, but somehow when it comes to football in particular, suddenly everyone is an expert even if they do not know what shape the ball is.

So the member of the Parliament decided to categorically post a message, urging the gods and demons to take matters into their own hands for Ranieri's crime in winning the Leicester title:

"To top it all off, Ranieri is mocking us; in interviews he gives in England, he comes right out and mocks us saying that he is the same man that was sacked by Greece. Ranieri forgot, of course, to refresh our memory about the fact that he is also the same man who grabbed a ton of money from the EPO, in a bankrupt country where he arrived with an air of absolute authority, took the national team of Greece from the threshold of the Mundial top 8, where they went with the honorable Mr. Santos, only to shred that accomplishment to pieces by taking the team to defeat by EVERYONE, even by the cod fishermen of the Faroe Islands, at the Karaiskaki stadium, ruining the worldwide prestige of the national team of Greece. He took the money and ran. Santos led Portugal to the EURO, but now we will watch everything from the comfort of our sofa, thanks to Ranieri.

"As for the English championship, Ranieri won the championship with the 100% dead City, Liverpool, Arsenal, United, and Chelsea. Their poor progress in Europe confirmed their lousiness. In such a dead English championship this year, even someone like Ranieri could win the title. Let's hear an official statement by someone from Ranieri's crew, since the EPO's masterminds have hidden themselves and are lazing about. Let's hear Kontonis say a few words about the national team being put to shame because of Ranieri, the Deputy Minister for Sport should not be crafty only in his own country."

One of the best reviews about Ranieri's stint in Greece was released by the website newsbomb.gr around the time the above post was written, and could have easily served as a reply. Kostas Skordoulis analyzes the events that took place during critical times in an article entitled "Ranieri, You Play Football Too Poorly for Wealthy Greece!"

"From the summer of 2014 and the relegation of the Greek national team to swooping to the top of the Premier League with little Leicester. Maybe in the end Ranieri was not to blame for the downfall of our Galanolefki (sky blue and white). The peddler, an unskilled maître d' of payouts? The person who managed to be defeated by the pizza guys of the Faroe Islands, and pin them to last place of their group in the qualification matches of the EURO 2016.

"Now, let's be honest, isn't this what nine out of ten people were saying and rejoicing over on November 15 when he was sacked from the Greek national team, just a day before our most humiliating defeat? Well, then, the 64-year-old Italian loser coach in a country with a population of 11 million people made history in a country with 53 million. But not against Romania, Northern Ireland, fishermen, and lawyers, but rather against Manchester United, Liverpool, Chelsea, Arsenal, Manchester City, Tottenham, and with players who do not speak the same language. The first question someone will ask is whether the national team is equal to the team you train every day with players on the field half of the day. The answer is of course not, but what Ranieri was able to do was make one of the most magnificent miracles in the history of football, and in its birthplace too. And to put it simply, Leicester rose up in the Premier League in the 2014-2015 season, for just 6 points they were not demoted (14th place) in the summer of 2015 the Italian sat on the bench of the foxes and is now champion of England!

"Can money buy success? NO!

"Money certainly would help you to do it, but that is not always the case. We will examine this with simple examples. Leicester is champion of England, Chelsea is excluded from Europe,

Manchester City is in the top three, and United is fighting for the Europa League. How much more simple can it be?

"Let's take a look at something even more interesting and let's speak in numbers. Claudio Ranieri's first official game on the bench of the Greek national team was on September 7, 2014. Defeated by Romania 1-0 in the Karaiskaki Stadium, the beginning of evil. Our national team's mission is estimated at about 83,355,000 GBP!**

"Let's examine the numbers more closely:

Karnezis	1,880,000
Kapino	1,500,000
Glikos	1,310,000
Manolas	9,750,000
Papastathopoulos	13,500,000
Torosidis	4,130,000
Tzavelas	1,500,000
Moras	525,000
K. Papadopolos	6,750,000
Vintra	750,000
A. Papadopoulos	2,400,000
Mandalos	938,000
Samaris	5,250,000
Tachtsidis	1,880,000
Fortsounis	900,000
Kone	4,500,000
Christodoulopoulos	1,500,000
Mitroglou	6,380,000
Samaras	2,250,000

Salpigidis	1,310,000
Athanasiadis	3,380,000
Diamantakos	1,130,000

"In the following two games, the national team was not able to savor any victory against Finland (1-1, away) nor against N. Ireland (0-2, home). Claudio Ranieri made some alterations, but the mission was still costly, 72,485,000 GBP** to be exact.

Karnezis	1,880,000
Kapino	1,500,000
Glikos	1,310,000
Manolas	9,750,000
Papastathopoulos	13,500,000
Torosidis	4,130,000
Stafilidis	1,500,000
Moras	525,000
Vintra	750,000
Scondras	1,500,000
Yannoulis	900,000
Mavrias	1,130,000
Mandalos	938,000
Samaris	5,250,000
Tachtsidis	1,880,000
Fortounis	900,000
Tziolis	900,000
Mitroglou	6,380,000
Samaras	2,250,000
Salpigidis	1,310,000
Athanasiadis	3,380,000
Karelis	1,130,000

CLAUDIO RANIERI – T(H)INKERMAN

"Let's go to the night of humiliation now, on November 14 at the Karaiskakis Stadium, where Greece was defeated by the Faroe Islands 1-0, a game that was the swan song of the 64-year-old Italian on the bench of the team. The players cost 47,498,000 GBP, but the fisherman, lawyers, and pizza men got the first win in their history of qualification matches for the EURO.

Karnezis	1,880,000
Kapino	1,500,000
Glikos	1,310,000
Manolas	9,750,000
Maniatis	3,750,000
Torosidis	4,130,000
Moras	525,000
Vintra	750,000
Karabelas	300,000
Bakakis	450,000
Tasoulis	225,000
A. Papadopoulos	2,400,000
Mavrias	1,130,000
Mandalos	938,000
Samaris	5,250,000
Tziolis	900,000
Kone	4,500,000
Christodoulopoulos	1,500,000
Kolovos	750,000
Dinas	450,000
Athanasiadis	3,380,000
Karelis	1,130,000
Gekas	600,000

"And now let's move on to the biggest surprise in the history of world football (on a club level), Leicester. We will not be discussing the present values because the Euro will have gone up. Let's go to the summer of 2015, when no one thought the Foxes were worth anything. In any case, it was the second favorite choice for relegation. Leicester, then, had an estimated worth of 62,118,000 GBP! Let's come to a conclusion. There are many adjectives in our vocabulary to call a coach who has trained teams such as Monaco, Inter, Roma, Juventus, Parma, Valencia, Chelsea, Atletico Madrid, Fiorentina and Napoli, and the words *failed* and *random* are not one of them. Actually, he would be described this way only in Greece. The coaches do not call stinks and we change coaches faster than the speed of light."

** The value of each player stated is based on the website transfermarkt, and always according to the value during that time and not the present value. The currency is GBP and not Euros.

15

The Metamorphosis of the Tinkerman

Claudio's mind was in a whirlwind. Rightfully so, because nothing was going according to his plan. His tension wasn't mounting due to the result of the match, but due to the way that Chelsea was losing vital points. He wasn't concerned about defeat as much as he wanted the team to apply what he had taught them on the pitch.

The first time someone referred to him as Tinkerman was when he was managing Chelsea. From then on, he was stuck with it. He wasn't pleased to be called the Tinkerman since it was not meant to be flattering. He was given this nickname because he was being ridiculed for his tactics. People—mostly the media—tried to use this name jokingly to describe the way he coached Chelsea. He would often switch the eleven players around from match to match and introduce many different players without having any rhyme or reason.

If the results had been good and Chelsea had performed as Ranieri—everyone else—wished, then no one would have mentioned it. The main question that did not concern anyone at the time was why he resorted to such measures in the first place.

The Metamorphosis of the Tinkerman

The atmosphere was as to be expected. He knew that he and he alone was the captain of the ship and therefore responsible for any failures. As John F. Kennedy said, "Victory has a thousand fathers, but defeat is an orphan."

During 2000-2004, he learned many of the biggest tricks of the trade. The main thing he learned is that patience and dedication are acquired through experience. These are qualities he and Leicester had and together they were able to work harmoniously during the 2015-2016 season. His tenure with Leicester had proven to be a school for him.

When he was referred to as the Tinkerman, he very often would stand his ground and say, "I will continue to make changes when they are necessary. That is my duty as a coach. A coach with very good players can make changes when he feels it is right. I want to play the football of the future, and for all of us in this line of work, it is time for a change."

He insisted on using this tactic. The trick was trying to pass on the mentality to his players. He had built this tactical system from his days of coaching amateur teams.

Ever since his time with the small club in Pozzuoli, he used the approach of changing the formation of the team during the matches. He always believed, and said quite often, that it was a good way to confuse the opponent during the match. Sometimes it worked, other times it didn't and he would leave the stadium defeated.

The time where he was like another Houdini and managed to change the balance of a team all by himself was on the bench of

Cagliari. Everyone was curious as to why he insisted on rotating the players of the team around. His reply was crystal clear. He saved Cagliari when he started to change the players around and when he kept them alert. He wanted them to understand that they were all valuable to the team and at any given time they may have to step in and help. This is the practice that made him a champion with Cagliari and brought him to Serie A.

"When I began changing the systems, nobody else was doing that in the Premier League. I was the first to do that then, but now many coaches do this and follow my example. All of Italy and England. Of course, then there's Gouardiola. When you play against his team, you do not know who the defender is if they play three, four, five at the back. It is always difficult to play against his team like that. You never know how he will play during the match," Claudio says.

Despite a long road full of obstacles along the way, he continued to be a true fighter, always a real survivor. There are some nice little stories in the black book of the Premier League; between 2000 and 2004, when Ranieri was with Chelsea, he used more than 50 players.

Only four teams have used more players through the years. From 2011-2015, eleven teams have used more players.

Queens Park Rangers	71
Sunderland	66
Fulham	60
Tottenham	60
Aston Villa	59
Chelsea	57
Arsenal	56

The Metamorphosis of the Tinkerman

Liverpool	55
Swansea City	55
West Bromwich	55
Manchester United	54

Over the next few years, his philosophy did not change dramatically with any of the teams he was appointed to. A short while before Claudio went to Leicester, he was accused of recruiting too many players to the national team of Greece in the four short months that he was their coach.

Whenever he is asked about his tactics, he is always very frank and speaks from his heart. Some years ago, he openly admitted that during the Champions League semifinals in 2004 with Monaco, he should have shuffled the players less. In this moment of sincerity, he confesses that he regretted the decision and should have handled things better so the team would not have been scored against twice at Stamford Bridge.

His parting with the Londoners was close at hand. The same night of the match, Roman Abramovich invited him to have dinner with him on his yacht. Claudio, who was always gracious, normally would not have refused such an invitation, but he did not attend, excusing himself by saying he was very tired. He knew all too well that his time was up and he had nothing more to offer English football by coaching Chelsea.

As fate, luck, and destiny would have it, and as everything in life changes, so would his nickname. Years later, the Tinkerman would become the Thinkerman; since being on the bench of Leicester, his manner of guiding the team and his determination made him king and champion of England.

The title Tinkerman has been cast off, and he is now affectionately known as the Thinkerman. For his historical win with the Foxes, he only used 23 players, with only 17 making over ten league appearances.

It really is a miracle if one considers the degree of difficulty an English championship has, and the necessity of having multiple options in such a harsh and competitive world such as that of British football. It is more than certain that he had carried the burden of being called the Tinkerman long enough.

A few days after winning the title with Leicester, he seized his opportunity. The time had come to change his trademark label and rename himself.

"I am the Thinkerman now, not Tinkerman!" he said to all who, for so many years, never missed an occasion to remind him of his Tinkerman stamp.

"To win the title in the Premier League is something special and even more special for Leicester. I am so happy, but even happier for these fantastic lads. It is unbelievable. I never even imagined this. We worked very hard. Everybody does, because that's how it is with English football, but in the end only one can win. This year it happened to me!"

From being mocked as the Tinkerman with Abramovich's Chelsea, Claudio Ranieri was El General for Valencia, Il Mister for Roma, and Dead Man Walking for Juventus and finally went on to title his book of memoirs of those years *Proud Man Walking*. All the proceeds of that book were donated to the Great Ormond Street Children's hospital for research.

Claudio was careful to be discrete about this and not to publicize it, which again shows his earnest character. This would not be the first time he participated in something for charity. He knows there is more to life than just football.

The ultimate justification for Thinkerman was now a reality. His new name, the title of the book you are reading, will be part of him eternally.

16

Ranieri Versus Mourinho

Claudio was driving toward London and, like most days, the weather was dull and rainy. While eating breakfast, he had the opportunity to glance at the daily newspapers. He was not bothered by the gloominess of the day's atmosphere but by the traffic in certain parts of the British capital, which can be extremely annoying at times; it can infuriate even the most relaxed person in the world.

Claudio had come to love London and the people in his life there. He is an affectionate man with everyone and enjoys bringing joy to everyone, especially his fans when they recognize him on the streets. If he is out and about and his fans spot him, he is always happy to take pictures and sign his autograph when asked.

It was midsummer 2003 when he started to plan for the following season with Chelsea. He was always planning ahead and organizing things he needed to do, which worked to his advantage many times.

His mobile phone chimed and it was Trevor Birch on the other end of the line. They had an appointment to make the arrangements for the new season. Chelsea's managing director always had barrage of information for him."Claudio, I have some important news."

Claudio remained silent, waiting to hear the details. "Roman Abramovich is officially the new owner of the team."

Claudio immediately spoke, "Trevor, my friend, this is it, we are the first to go." He was certain that one of the first things Abramovich would do would be to get rid of him and most of the team's staff as well.

But we should never say never in life, and the same applies to football; you never know how things will pan out. Ranieri remained with the team for exactly a year after that telephone conversation with Trevor. He was as surprised as everyone else, because he did not expect they would be staying that much longer. He later commented on that.

"I was sure, it was almost certain, that Abramovich would sack me as soon as he became the owner of Chelsea. When Trevor Birch informed me, I knew very well that we would be the first to go home. We had an appointment with Trevor that day to plan the new season, but my first words when he told me were 'you and I are the first to go.' It is normal for the new owner of a team to keep his own men."

Coaches are like lawyers. People like to change them. New owners like to bring an air of change to a team as well. In order for a new era to begin for Mourinho on Chelsea's bench, it was necessary for Ranieri to lend a helping hand. Abramovich's investment seemed unreal, not only according to Premier League standards, but according to the entire football world. In the summer of 2003, the Russian billionaire spent approximately 190,000,000 EUR on an English football team, without thinking twice about it. Claudio Ranieri played the leading role in the deal and maybe this was the reason that Roman Abramovich kept him on the bench of the team the first year.

The foundations had been put down the previous season. The year Mourinho was appointed topped it all off. Ranieri had done all the planning for an excellent team and defense strategy. The way it worked on the field was the envy of all. But he was missing players with integrity and personality that would hoist the team to the top. He knew what the team needed, so he already knew who he wanted to recruit.

The team needed a great striker, a fantastic winger, and a successful goalkeeper. He wanted to recruit three specific players to make up the backbone of the team. In Claudio's mind, Didier Drogba was a killer in the opponent's box. He had seen enough with Olympique Marseille to know that he was ready to take the team a step up.

Dutchman Arjen Robben was like a machine with a computer chip in his left leg. He was already a bone of contention, a matter of dispute for Barcelona and Real Madrid. He is a fantastic player, ready to do great things in the Premier League. There weren't many significant goalkeepers in the market at the time for what Claudio was scouting to play for Chelsea. Petr Cech, a tower beneath the goal posts at a height of 1.96 meters, had played for the French club Rennes, and was already international. Ranieri believed he would be perfect for Chelsea. They were the three players that changed the history of the team. Claudio left, and the players were recruited.

Mourinho was on the bench now, and he was the one who experienced the championship win the following season, something Chelsea had waited years for. Claudio said:

"I am certain now and I can say for sure that during my third season we performed very well. Without signing players, we placed fourth, the best place of any other time, after many years.

"What we achieved in the Champions League was the reason Roman Abramovich bought the team. We placed second in the Premier League, after Arsenal, the team that was undefeated that season, and arrived to the Champions League semifinals. I had found some great players, players with potential. I very much believed that we could reach the top with them. The players were Petr Cech and Arjen Robben. I had also spoken to Abramovich about Didier Drogba, when he asked who I would want for a striker if I were to stay. The truth is that the season before I wanted Samuel Eto'o, I liked him, he was a fighter and scorer as well, and moved a lot on the pitch, he worked for the team. But it was not possible to bring him, so I chose Drogba. But when Drogba arrived, I had already been sacked."

Claudio always took to heart the fact that he built the foundations that made Chelsea stronger and Mourinho never thanked him for everything he had done to prepare the team. The Italian had provided for the greatest players to come to Stamford Bridge.

Abramovich's great desire was to appoint Eriksson to Chelsea. In the back of his mind, Abramovich always held Claudio's opinion in high regard, because he appreciated him. They were never friends and they never socialized because their relationship was highly professional. The Russian often emphasized to Ranieri that Chelsea was his home and the door would always be open to him for whatever he needed.

CLAUDIO RANIERI – T(H)INKERMAN

Later the feud between Mourinho and Ranieri became more epic. Not only did Mourinho not say thank you to Ranieri, but he took a jab at him every chance he had. This Portuguese man has an arrogant nature and does not leave well enough alone. Anyone who dared to provoke him with public comments were really in for it.

In his farewell interview from Chelsea, Ranieri said he did not believe Mourinho could survive in the Premier League. He did not mean it insultingly, but meant that there were many difficulties for a coach with Mourinho's performances to face in the hard and relentless world of British football.

It was said based on Ranieri's own experiences from his tenure on the bench of a British team, especially a team such as Chelsea. Not only was it difficult, it was practically impossible to withstand all the pressure. Mourinho had substantial European successes with Porto.

At that time, he was not expressing bitterness towards Mourinho, but mainly about the way he was bidding farewell to Chelsea. He had been through difficult years and managed to build a team by choosing players that could easily make the difference to take the team up a step. In the midst of his greatest moment, someone else was taking over his own creation, and would be stealing all the glory. This alone can cause one to react in such a way that's only human.

Mourinho did not miss the chance to respond to Claudio's statements: "Yes, I heard that and what I suggest is that if any one of you are friends with Ranieri and have his number, you should ring him up and explain that for a team to win the European Cup, you have to play many times against teams from different countries. I did not win the cup playing against 20 Portuguese teams; I played and I defeated clubs from his country, the country in which he worked, in England, and all of Europe."

The Italian had a naturally calm demeanor and above all he does not lose his temper. He wanted to bury the hatchet after that. There was no sense in locking horns with Mourinho. He had never done this with anyone and he would not be doing it now. He knew all too well who he was and said he would not be able to have anything to do with Mourinho. They were two different personalities and he knew that he didn't need validation from anyone. He had already had a career in European football.

"I am not like Mourinho; I don't have to win things to be sure of myself," Ranieri said, and naturally he received a reply from his foe.

"I guess he's right with what he said, I am very demanding of myself and I have to win to be sure of things. This is why I have won so many trophies in my career. Ranieri, on the other hand, has the mentality of someone who doesn't need to win. He is almost 70 years old, he has won a Super Cup and another small trophy, and he is too old to change his mentality. He's old and he hasn't won anything. I studied Italian five hours a day for many months to ensure I could communicate with the players, the media, and the fans. Ranieri has been in England for five years and still struggles to say good morning and good afternoon."

The battles did not stop and when they met again at the Italian championship, it was like Sodom and Gomorrah.

In 2010, when Ranieri's Roma was just before the home stretch of the championship finale, four points ahead of Mourinho's Inter, the Portuguese coach suggested to the competitors below Roma to offer their bonus to Siena, which was one of Roma's next opponents. Ranieri was angered by what Mourinho had blatantly suggested, and said:

"You all think Mourinho is a phenomenon? No, he is not. It is the media that gives him that aura. For me he is a good coach and I won't say anything more. The way he's playing is not the kind of football I like and neither do the people. Just as I like respect, I give respect. It's easy to motivate a team feeling under attack from everyone. Sport is an important vehicle for Italian society. Behaving like this launches time bombs. I am a man of sport and I like football and I will serve football until the end."

The two contenders' teams were up against each other at the Italian final. Mourinho was the winner. Wanting to get a rise out of the Italian coach once more, he said he had watched six different games to find Roma's weaknesses and commented on the difference in the way they both prepared their teams for the final.

"Before the final, I spent three hours on each game. Of course, it's easier to just watch a movie in the cinema, but Ranieri has forgotten his players are champions, not children. If before a match I did something like that, my players would die laughing, or they would call the doctor to see if I were ill."

This was because Claudio chose to see *Gladiator* with his players before the big final.

Their clashes have gone on for years and many things started up during the 2004 season, when Mourinho said, "It is not my fault if in 2004 I replaced him and said that the team wanted to win and with him that would never happen. It's not my fault they think he is a loser."

Yet, again, life plays strange games. The man Mourinho considered a loser was crowned champion of England during the 2015-2016 season. The war ended when Ranieri returned to Italy in 2011 and Mourinho was the first to send him a welcome message. They met and agreed to call a truce.

"When I was with Inter, he would send me a message every week. He's a nice boy."

The days of hostility were a thing of the past. Love had prevailed. Ranieri stated that their clashes were behind them. Once again, he spoke from his soul.

"In this competition you cannot be friends, but you have to change a few words."

He called Mourinho to wish him luck when he took over Inter. There would be peace now. The Portuguese coach had put a feather in his cap and praised Ranieri for Leicester winning the championship.

"I want to congratulate everyone in Leicester City Football Club, players, staff, owners and fans. I lost my title to Claudio Ranieri and it is with incredible emotion that I live this magic moment in his career."

The fact that Ranieri's best moment coincided with Mourinho's worst season in the Premier League is no longer of importance.

17

On the Road to a Miracle

On a list of all-time bests in the history of the Premier League, there are several reasons why one would mention Claudio Ranieri's name. Minutes after winning the title with Leicester, everyone was searching to find out how he and his lads prevailed.

In the history of the Premier League, he is the coach who set the record for quickest ever title win. From the day he was appointed to the bench of Leicester and became the trailblazer of Leicester's efforts for the 2015-2016 season, it took only 294 days from the morning of July 3, 2015 until the day he grasped the golden ticket in his hands to take Leicester to a the land of miraculous victory. It was the newest record for the most rapid title conquest in Great Britain.

He broke Mourinho's record from the 2005-2006 season, where 332 days were needed for him to be crowned the champion in his first tenure on the English pitches with Chelsea. The same Chelsea that Ranieri created.

Mourinho, of course, has the honor of being in the top five twice for the least days needed to win a trophy. Carlo Ancelloti, champion with Chelsea in 2010, needed 342 days to be crowned champion. Arsene Wenger took 579 days from the day he was appointed to Arsenal to winning the championship in the 1995-1996 season. Ranieri's trip over these 294 days was not all smooth sailing. He had to fight in stormy seas for 294 days until he reached his goal.

August 2015: Against All Odds From Day One

A good beginning will bring success and this may apply to many events of our everyday life. In football, the season is like a marathon; the race begins in summer, the course passes through autumn's evaluations, winter is the great uphill challenge, and spring is the finish line. The course may lead to paradise. In August 2015, when the most thrilling season in Ranieri's coaching career began, nobody—not even Ranieri himself—could have imagined that he would be the one to pass the finish line to paradise.

Many viewed his appointment with much skepticism and criticized the choice Leicester's people made to recruit him to the bench. Critics thought a 64-year-old coach had no business trying to get a title.

Opening day began with the performance of rock group Kasabian, whose music was used to inspire the team. Opening day was magical on August 8, 2015 at King Power Stadium. It was a humid day and temperatures had risen. The players' uniforms were clinging to their bodies from the heat. Leicester's 32,242 fans had tightly packed into the stadium to watch the Foxes play. A few minutes after the kickoff, Jamie Vardy did what he knew how to do better than anyone else. He would repeat it many times during the season.

At the eleventh minute, he scored, triggering a chain reaction in a season of goals. On that day, Riyad Mahrez decorated his path on the halfway line and was a star performer as well as a passer. He scored two goals, one through a penalty kick. Marc Albrighton finished off the magical premier. The match ended with Leicester defeating Sunderland with a score of 4-2. It was only the beginning of a series of wins. Kasabian's song "Fire" was what Claudio used to inspire the team without missing a beat. "When we hear the song 'Fire' by Kasabian, that means we become warriors."

Excellent in public relations, he began to whip up excitement right away. He knew exactly how to do it and during the following season, he continued to do it masterfully. He had become accustomed to the city and its lifestyle. He wanted to have his slice of the city from early on. He never pretended to be something he wasn't. More than anything, he wanted to be himself in his new endeavour.

Serge, the guitarist of Kasabian, seized the moment and said, "After hearing Ranieri's words I think that's up there with the ultimate, I could give up all my awards up for that."

Ranieri had become very popular even before the matches of the season had begun. People realized this as time passed. The first step had been taken and his personality helped everything fall into place. He entered gracefully. He was fearless and had faith in everyone. They mirrored it all back to him with new positive energy. The results were quick to show.

A week later, Leicester faced a great challenge with West Ham. Payet and his crew awaited Ranieri's lads in London. Destiny reared its head up early and just like in the first game against

Sunderland, Mahrez scored again. Of course, no one could fathom what would follow. Eleven minutes after Mahrez scored, Shinji Okazaki put Leicester in the lead.

It was their second match and their second win, two out of two, and they had barely even started. The month of August ended with two 1-1 draws, one with Tottenham and the other with Bournemouth. The season had begun ideally, even better than anyone had dreamed.

September 2015: You Old Fox

Youth is exuberance, old age experience. Throughout his grand path through King Powers, it never crossed Claudio's mind that in August he had been considered an old man. The championship was underway and Leicester began to show that something good was happening. It wasn't just the results.

Two wins and two draws from the get-go—and in difficult matches—were encouraging results. Those who had criticized his age or his coaching ways began to think twice.

Once in a debate, former US president Ronald Reagan was asked about his age and about the fact that he was the oldest president of the United States. It did not take long for him to answer the concerned host's question, and he quipped, "I will not exploit my opponent's youth and inexperience for political purposes."

You old fox.

Claudio responded in a similar way. He knew how to make an impression and knew how to seize the moment. Sixteen teams, one of which was a national team, in a thirty-year career. Thirty years around the globe. With images and experiences that could not be discredited, and erased all at once. He thought, "That should be respected dammit. They can't blame me because of my experience!" He lived in some of the most brilliant parts of Europe.

Monaco, Milan, London, Madrid. It could not all just be wiped away. It could not be just thrown away by those who wanted to believe different things about him without even knowing him. The season had started very well and the foundations had been put down.

"I like to travel. I like to discover new places. I am like Christopher Columbus." Everyone silently waited

The victory over Aston Villa with a score of 3-2, on September 13, 2015, sent a strong message to all. Leicester was the second on the tables, behind City and above United and Arsenal. At the Britannia, six days later, Stoke City proved to be tough. The usual suspects, Mahrez and Vardy, were the scorers of the match, but the final result of a 2-2 draw was to be an omen of the crisis ahead. The fans were living in their own dream world, the betting companies started to make their own scenarios, some were fantasizing about the far future, even about leaving Europe, but the first big test for Claudio's team was ahead.

He knew that everyone thought the team started off with a bang and what really mattered was for it to last. He thought that the team should be relaxed without feeling pressure about the next important match, which would be at home with Arsenal, one of the traditional favorites for the 2015-2016 season.

Wenger was impressed by the team's successful start and by how skillfully Leicester played. He even stated that the match at King Power would not be easy because the way Leicester plays, they can be dangerous to a team with their capabilities.

The match was amazing, but that afternoon Jamie Vardy was robbed of his glory by Alexis Sanchez. Vardy put Leicester in the lead from early on, just 13 minutes into the match, but Arsenal started a stunning avalanche. Sanchez scored a hat trick bringing the final score to 2-5, in Arsenal's favor. Quite a loud slap in the face for Claudio and his players.

It was a rough landing and the clouds of pessimism filled the sky over King Power again. Even with the wins, the defense was scathed, and the team needed to watch its back and proceed to counterattack more cautiously. The match with the Gunners revealed several weaknesses. The negative reviews resurfaced again and everyone started to talk about how the first five competitions were just fireworks.

He answered in his own way. He let his players rest to clear their minds.

October 2015: Welcome, Thinkerman

He recognized the fact that the team needed something along the lines of shock therapy for their behavior to change. He did not have much room for changes to reshape things for his team.

The Tinkerman had won people's hearts and had become the man who thinks, the Thinkerman. First his own survival instinct had to kick in and then the team's. He knew that in the wild world of

British football the moment is everything. A victory could restore the good atmosphere, just like a defeat could shatter a good impression.

The marathon had just begun. Of course, no one could judge who the winner would be right away. But his sharks—as he liked to call the reporters—had already begun to hunt. They caught the scent of Claudio's blood and he became their first and easiest prey. They had been eyeing their prey since the beginning of the season when it was announced that he had been appointed to Leicester. He was the first person they would devour if something went wrong. The skies were darkening over Leicester's bright start. In the beginning of October 2015, management tactics were critical. He thought of different tricks every day to keep his players alert.

Around that time, he thought of pizza and its health benefits, as well as the culinary delight it offered. He promised his players that, for every match that no goals were scored against them, he would treat them to as much pizza as they wished. Fostering a spirit of solidarity and brotherliness was the deeper reason behind this idea. They would all be doing something together and he wanted to bring them closer to each other this way. To have a feeling of togetherness. Initially he was vehemently criticized for this new idea. Some, who just wanted to find fault in him, found ways to pick apart his gesture and ridicule him. But he and his players were not easily discouraged. They knew what their goal was.

October was a difficult month, or at least it seemed so after Leicester was defeated by Arsenal. At Carrow Road, Norwich did not stand a chance to stop Leicester's comeback to the winner's

On the Road to a Miracle

circle, and Vardy found his way back to the nets again. The victory gave wings to the team again and the players' faith was restored.

Claudio knew that the next three games were decisive in order for Leicester to remain at the top of the charts. He was concerned because the team was being scored against. It happened in the match with Southampton, especially in the first half of the game. It was a matter of concentration, not the defenders' competence. It was not a matter of fatigue or negligence during the match either.

He saw his team being scored against in neutral zones, where the opponent normally would not have the initiative during the match, and that made him think. He knew the team had to work on their concentration skills, so he worked with them every day during training.

The match with Southampton ended in a draw and Leicester slid to fifth place, so everyone started to consider that sooner or later the team would be going downhill. Some members of the team became frustrated, but Claudio had to keep his cool and make wise decisions about the future. And he definitely did.

He knew of a way to make it happen. Before Leicester's home game against Crystal Palace, he reminded the players about their bet. If no goals were scored against them, they would all be going to Peter's pizzeria in the center of Leicester for a treat. Free pizza on Claudio for all.

Crystal Palace proved to be easy prey and 32,000 Leicester fans celebrated as another goal was scored by Vardy, who was on a smashing goal-scoring streak.

The players made pizza dough and some of them, like Okazaki and Fuch, proved to be very skilled at it. They laughed to their heart's content and were brought closer together.

November 2015: Bionic Jamie

Everyone was talking about bionic Jamie, who was breaking one record after another. Ranieri's locomotive stopped nowhere, and all of the media and sports fans had turned their attention to Leicester and Vardy. He managed to do something, which at the beginning of the season seemed impossible. He scored unfailingly in eleven consecutive matches. He began to write his own history and broke Ruud Van Nistelrooy's previous record.

In the back of his mind, Claudio was working on various strategy scenarios. The season had started well and the team had pushed to the top five. Clearly he would not be having bigger dreams at that time. He was a realist. He began to slowly trust his intuition. He was never really superstitious. He always believed in signs and intuition, though, and this had helped him to reach some wise decisions in his career as with Madrid and Atletico, and eccentric Gil, where he walked away before he was sacked.

Before every press conference, he always shakes the hand of not only the reporters in the room, but also of the technicians as well. Before he sits down to analyze a match, he walks around the room greeting everyone.

Each and every person in the room is greeted individually. Time is of no concern. He never snubs anyone. This is a habit he enforces in the locker room, with all his teams, before every match or training session.

When he was with the national team of Greece, some of the players would scoff at this. He thought differently, outside the box, outside of the ordinary.

Vardy had his weapon on the pitch. Jamie was voted player of the month in October of 2015, and in November he had the honor again, but this time with his coach by his side. Claudio and Jamie scooped up awards together for best player and manager in the Premier League. They would have more such achievements in the future, but at that point in time they were the stars of the show.

Jamie scored in consecutive matches against Watford, Newcastle, and Manchester United, which is when he broke the record for scoring in eleven games straight. Two wins and one draw in the month of November brought waves of excitement. Leicester was consistent in bringing results even on the nights that they did not perform well.

Claudio was over the moon. "I am very, very happy. We wanted the win today, but we also wanted to help Jamie to achieve the record. Well done to my players for helping Vardy to score. The whole team is in very good physical condition and they have a good mentality."

He had all his players work to support the personal interest of one player, Jamie. He did not use clichéd words such as "everyone is equal on the team" and "no one stands out" but instead he taught them that they are all for one and one for all.

December 2015: Dilly Ding Dilly Dong!

The Christmas season in Britain is a wonderful time of the year. Boxing Day, the day after Christmas, is the highlight that the football fans to look forward to because a number of football matches take place on that day.

The evening of December 5, 2015, found Leicester at the top of the charts, two points ahead of Arsenal, and three ahead of Manchester, City, and United. Just a few hours ago, Riyad Mahrez was on a hat-trick spree and the score was 3-0 in the match against Swansea. The Algerian took over for Vardy, who was taking a break from his own scoring spree of 11 matches in a row with nonstop hammering into the nets of the opposition.

Before the match, Claudio, like everyone else in Leicester, had his attention turned to Jamie, who was ready to reinforce his record. However, Riyadh was the striker and Vardy was the passer. At the end of the match, Ranieri kept a conservative outlook, saying that 40 points was the objective, but that they must remain calm with their feet on the ground.

A few days later, he played the role of Father Christmas for his players and the staff. One morning, he went to the shops by himself and purchased 30 bells, one for each of them. The cashier gave him a puzzled look, but she did not ask him what he would do with so many bells. Then he exclaimed, "Dilly ding! Dilly dong!" and everyone burst out laughing, but not everyone knew what he meant. This became his new catchphrase.

When the players were in the changing room, he gave them each a bell, and the training session took on a very festive mood. Claudio shouted at them gleefully, "Dilly ding! Dilly dong! Wake up, something good is happening. It's far, but we can see it."

He bought those bells for all of them as a gift, to keep them alert. In his own unique way, without putting them under pressure, he

On the Road to a Miracle

was giving them the message that they needed to concentrate. He knew that choosing to do it in this way made it more heartfelt. The players received the message and knew what he was asking of them.

On December 14, a cold and damp Monday night by the icy lake next to King Power, Leicester was waiting to welcome Chelsea. It was a special match and he knew that it would be the first of many big steps that the team would have to take if they wanted to live their dream. In the days before the match, for the first time, he set an objective for Leicester to play outside of Europe.

This was a very big deal for the club, which up until a few years ago had been at the bottom of the barrel. Nobody can say for sure if he had something else in mind. When I met him in Leicester, in March, after the important win over Newcastle, he gave the impression that his mission had been accomplished. You could tell that he was enjoying himself, but I'm sure he was already thinking about the title. It was a good trick to make his interviewer feel at ease and have things move along smoothly. It's certain now that, even before Christmas of 2015, he'd begun to think about winning the magic title, but he was strategically taking things slow.

Again, life was up to its usual strange games and Leicester defeated Mourinho's Chelsea, which was kicked down to 16th place. It was Claudio's finest moment being on top, and his now friend Jose watched Chelsea dip toward the relegation zone.

"Dilly ding, dilly dong, we are in the Champions League!" could be heard from the changing rooms of the team. He was laughing wholeheartedly. He was sure that the road had opened and it would only lead toward the sky.

On Boxing Day, he'd already figured out that if the results were positive, he would have a voice. Then with the matches with Everton, Liverpool, and Manchester City at King Power throughout the year, he noticed that people had begun to treat him differently.

On December 19, 2015, at Goodison Park, the evening belonged entirely to Riyad Mahrez aka the Arabian Stallion and his nerves of steel, where he scored twice from the penalty box, gaining three points against Everton.

Everybody in Great Britain was talking about the miracle of the underdog, Leicester. On Christmas Day the previous year (2014), the Foxes had been in last place, and now they were on top with Arsenal in second and Manchester City third.

Before the game with Everton, Claudio was worried about Vardy, who had an injured hamstring, but Leicester's sports doctors stepped in. Another one of the many miracles of the season. In the end, Ranieri set the target of forty points that would ensure they would remain, but everyone was aware that he knew how to play this game well. That Christmas was one of the best of his life. He was first in the Premier League with a five-point difference and he was ready for new adventures.

Being defeated by Liverpool cannot be considered such a slap in the face, especially when you are playing in Anfield. Everyone in Leicester knew very well that the matches with Liverpool and City could create a certain climate for the continuation. Leicester fell from the top and Claudio said, "Every match is difficult for us. This league is very crazy. Maybe nobody wants to win the title. It's very strange. We're the basement and the other teams

On the Road to a Miracle

are a villa with a swimming pool. It's not easy for us. What we're doing is miraculous."

He'd started to set the framework and put things in their true form.

January 2016: Claudio Got His Gun

Kicking off the new year with a 0-0 draw with Bournemouth at King Power, everyone thought that Leicester was beginning to deflate. Everyone except Claudio, that is. He knew how to keep the players and the media intact.

In the press room, after the match ended in a draw, he faced the moment smoothly, and did not miss his opportunity. He spoke in numbers with the reporters, and said that with the 39 points from the first round of the championship, the goal would be to improve and gather the points in the second round.

One of his sharks asked him, "So your target is set for 80 points before the final?"

"No, 79," he fired back.

He knew how to play with them, and he had his answers ready. Leicester made history when they gathered 79 points out of 81 total and celebrated winning the title.

After starting off on the wrong foot at the beginning of January 2016, the great win over Tottenham 0-1 at White Hart Lane marked the counterattack. At Villa Park, Okazaki gave them the precious draw point against Aston Villa, and a week later Drinkwater, Vardy, and Ulloa successively scored against Stoke.

The Foxes were on their way to a triumphant comeback.

By the end of January, you could see the championship faintly approaching in the distance.

February 2016: Happy Days

They had accomplished their goal.

"Our pressure was to save the team. We saved the team, you see? Now we must enjoy it. Match after match, step by step. Now this league is so strange. Nobody knows who can win it."

That was all it took; it was like a weight was magically lifted from the players. Fate was predetermined and everyone in Etihad Stadium of Manchester knew it by noon on February 6.

Huth put them in an early lead within the first three minutes. From then on, it was blast off! The 1-3 victory against Manchester City was a significant win, and Leicester moved five points from Tottenham, who had an equally impressive year. Ranieri started to be more assertive with the opponents, but also with the football fans. After the end of the match he gave a statement to the BBC:

"We played without pressure because we don't have to win the league. We must enjoy it to the very end and live the moment! This league is so strange and now it is important to think about Arsenal. I want to wait until the end of April because I know the last matches are very tough. This is a fantastic moment for the Premier League, nobody knows who can win it."

Ranieri knew that the only way they would be able to go all the way was if his players were not tense. The next day he gave an interview to the *Corrier Della Sera* and tipped the scales with what he said to everyone in the football world. He surprised even the most die-hard fans of the sport. It was the first time he unveiled some of his secrets, but he also spoke about his relationship with his players.

"When I first arrived to Leicester, from the first training days I immediately realized that the players did not like my tactical approaches, so I told them that I would not exhaust them with such things. I do not demand a lot, I only want them to do basic things, but what is most important is for them to run hard. Every Sunday, after the match, but also every Wednesday, they are free to do whatever they please."

During that interview, Claudio also spoke about how shocked he was the first time he saw his players eat and discovered what a hearty appetite they had.

"The first time we sat down at the dinner table together, I was shocked by how much they eat. I could not do anything but allow them to eat what as much as they want, and whatever they want, as long as they give me 100% during training and the matches."

By Valentine's Day, Arsenal had become the biggest obstacle for the Italian's squad. The atmosphere of the Emirates Stadium was festive, and 60,000 football fans saw Vardy giving Leicester the lead from the penalty box at the stroke of the first half. It seemed as if half the job had been done, but never say never in life and never say never in football either.

CLAUDIO RANIERI – T(H)INKERMAN

Ranieri's lads were fighting like lions and Schmeichel was chasing away anything coming into his den. But after Wolcott's equalizer 70 minutes into the game, during extra time, Welbeck caught a magnificent header off of Ozil's free kick and scored, grabbing those three points on behalf of Arsenal.

He was annoyed with Atkinson, the referee, for sending Simpson off with two yellow cards. He said that the referee was under pressure and two yellow cards were an extreme reaction. Still he congratulated Arsenal for a job well done.

The defeat did not really faze him because he had his own agenda. He gave his players a week off from training and all of Europe was in awe. The news circulated around the world as it was unthinkable for a coach of a pioneering team to decide to give his players a week of leave midseason in the toughest league of the world.

The scene was quite surreal, as experts from around the world began to accuse Ranieri of practices that were contrary to what everyone knew. The players did not let the opportunity go to waste and they left Leicester with their families so as to take advantage of the mini holiday that their coach so generously offered them. Some went to Dubai for a change of climate, and a group of them—lead by their goalkeeper, Kasper Schmeichel—spent five dream days in Copenhagen.

Claudio stayed in London for a day, and then took a trip to Rome to enjoy his coffee in the Eternal City at the expense of those who criticized him for allowing his players to take time off. There were twelve fixtures left until the final and he was just two points away from everyone else. He knew exactly what he was doing. The sin of sending his players on holiday for a week changed the common training methods of football worldwide.

Over the next twelve weeks Leicester was be a highspeed train, winning eight of the twelve games remaining, with four draws. There was one match, a final round with Chelsea, which did not have any significant point value since the Foxes had already celebrated the championship earlier.

March 2016: Like Obama and Castro

He was enjoying life and his work more than ever. His mission was complete almost ten weeks before the Premier League even finished, and whatever was going to happen after that, he knew he was already the champion of the season.

When I got to meet him in the middle of March 2016, a few weeks before Leicester won the title, he was on top of the world and you felt it from the very first moment you entered the room. He always was a very positive person, but now his eyes were shining in anticipation for the extraordinary event, which was about to occur.

Leicester's course and Ranieri's conduct became the main topic for discussion in the football world. Our meeting was on March 15 at Leicester's training facilities. I had been through quite a struggle to be able to meet with him because the hardest thing to do at that point in time was to make an appointment to see him for a chat. He was currently the man of the hour in football and everyone wanted to interview him. His popularity could be compared to that of Barack Obama, or Fidel Castro, and you had to book the appointment a long time in advance to get permission to see him. In a separate chapter, there is an analysis of how both my interviews with Ranieri took place, and what was needed in order to have the honor.

The match that ended in a draw with West Brom—but also the victory with Watford in early March 2016—took Leicester to the final with Newcastle at King Power. Newcastle's manager, Rafa Benitez, had just been appointed.

Before the match, I met Emile Heskey at the VIP entrance of King Power. He knew what an exciting time it was. He gave us a statement: "Yes, we are living a miracle. It is true, a few matches before the final no one expected we would come to this. They deserve a lot of credit and congratulations are in order, especially to Claudio Ranieri for a fantastic job."

Leicester was all over the pitch in the match against Newcastle and many believed that things would not be easy that night. Okazaki did his amazing acrobatic overhead kick, scoring probably the best goal of the 2015-2016 season. The next day Claudio was absolutely glowing with pride during our interview.

"It is a very special year. The chairman asked me if we could stay in the same division the next season, but things turned out even better. I do not know if there is a special secret. The secret is the good atmosphere in the changing room with the players, the staff of the team, and the supporters.

"I do not know if this has been the best season of my career. Up until now, it has not been, because I have also taken many smaller teams to second place. The initial target was to save the team and now it is to go to the Europa League. Our next target is the

Champions League. Right now we are in a good place and it is important to win one match at a time. I do not have dreams. I think first about the job that needs to be done and how we can improve. I have not regretted that I coached the Greek national team. It was a strange time. I was trying new things by taking on a national team. I was not able to build something of my own because I had no time. We only played four games. It was difficult. Many people tell me to write a book. For now, football is my priority. My time in Greece was not bad. I always loved Greece and I always will. The Greek people are fantastic. I hope that the Greeks will have many successes. They are wonderful and warm people. I wish them luck."

The month of March ended with an important win of 1-0 for Leicester. Ranieri's lads did exactly what they had to do against Crystal Palace and that is why they left the stadium victorious.

April 2016: Tears of a Lifetime

He was calm—or maybe he only *looked* as if he were composed—because he had to be. He knew that he was the one that had to keep it together. Everyone around the world was talking about what was about to happen.

From everything that was happening, Ranieri had all the excitement built up inside him. He knew his moment had come. It was a moment that he had dreamed about many years before but he had never truly lived it to the full extent. He wanted to conquer the championship.

In early April, Wes Morgan scored against Southampton and gave Leicester their fifth consecutive win of 1-0. The Foxes launched to the top of the tables, 7 points ahead of Tottenham, and 11 ahead of Arsenal. N'golo Kante played an amazing game and kept Leicester upright.

Claudio felt that the job was almost done. He remained cool and at the end he played the game he knew, saying that the team was just fighting for a place that would take them to Europe and the Champions League.

The most powerful image of the 2015-2016 season was of Claudio Ranieri after the match against Allardyce's Sunderland. The Sky Sports camera focused on him and Ranieri was unable to hold back his tears. It was a very emotional image of a man, who had struggled for many years to achieve the ultimate only to find his efforts thwarted.

Sensitive, with principles and dignity, he broke down and released all of his emotions. The image was shown around the world and became a symbol of faith and power for Leicester supporters, but mainly for his players. The image pulled on the heartstrings of many, even those who are not usually emotional. He had won everyone's hearts.

Defeating Sunderland meant the opening bell for the championship. Leicester needed only three wins to catch the dream. Vardy was unstoppable, scoring one goal after another. Ranieri made a statement to BBC Sports:

"The fans can dream, but we must remain calm. We are very close to the title of the Premier League with this match, but we still have a long way to go and we must work."

On the Road to a Miracle

Of course, he was asked about his tears of joy when the match was over.

"It is difficult to tell you how I feel at this moment. Everybody can dream, but we must stay focused on our goal. We have to remain calm, and continue with stability. Today we made many mistakes and we have to see what we did wrong, and improve."

The star of the show in the great match against West Ham was to be referee Moss, who came under fire because he sent off Jamie Vardy on the 56th minute of the game. It was the main topic of discussion for many days.

The game seemed lost and Claudio felt his demons pursuing him again five matches before the final. He kept his composure and made his checkmate move. The initial shock was followed by the kiss of life that Ulloa gave in the 95th minute by scoring from the penalty spot and saving Leicester with a dramatic draw in a match that seemed already lost.

The hot topic of Vardy missing had everyone waiting to see what Ranieri would do to replace the player, who had scored 22 goals that season.

He knew what to say in his first interview the day after the game with West Ham. He said Leicester had very good players he could depend on, and one of them was the Argentinean Jose Leonardo Ulloa, a strong tower of a forward. He had been Ranieri's secret weapon for that match.

Before the match, Claudio gave a helping hand to Ulloa to push his spirits high and make him feel as if he was the strongest man in the world. For Claudio, at that moment, he was indeed, even though Ulloa was not his first choice.

At the end of April, the game with Swansea appeared as if it would be a run-of-the-mill kind of game. Well, four goals and innumerable fantastic moves later, the air smelled of Leicester champions. It was anything but a standard game. Ulloa was flying on the pitch and did everything imaginable; he even scored twice.

Leicester was on the way to the theater of dreams to play the biggest role in its history, to face the biggest challenge of all. The team would fight for 90 minutes and try and conquer the biggest football title in all of Great Britain.

May 2016: A Mother's Blessing

The statement Wes Morgan made about the players being like brothers touched hearts. It was true, most times after a match you would see the Leicester players leaving King Power together, sometimes two or three in one car. They were very familiar with each other, like family. They were all as one. Their friendly banter followed them outside the changing room as well, with Vardy joking around with N'golo Kante and Okazaki, always smiling and good natured.

Ranieri's contribution to the climate was very hands-on in the way he treated everyone from the very first day he met the players. The cherry on top of the cake was when the final game between Tottenham and Chelsea ended in a draw. Jamie Vardy invited the whole gang over to his home to watch the game of their lives. When the final whistle blew, the whole squad fell on each other into a heap on Vardy's living room floor after realizing they won the league.

Claudio did not watch the game between Chelsea and Tottenham. On the day of the match, which would determine if Leicester was going to be the champion or not, he traveled to Italy to visit his beloved mother for her 96th birthday, thus showing his compassionate side. Perhaps for his own peace of mind he chose to be with his mother instead of watching the match, as a type of personal psychotherapy.

He fully respected family values and always had from when he was very young. His wife and children came first and then everything else. He did not let his own needs get in the way of spending time with his family. He was not a vain man. He was celebrating with his mama instead of watching the match that made him champion of England. He wanted to live special moments with the people who supported him through difficult times. The players were his children and his family was like his big brother looking out for him.

In the 2015-2016 season, Chelsea, the team that he had been discouraged by, had now compensated him for this by giving him the opportunity to celebrate the title in all of its glory. That's life. Sometimes you fly and sometimes you crash into harsh reality. The season came to an end and he wore a medal upon his chest and held the precious Premier League Cup in his arms. Claudio sealed his presence on the world football map forever and went down in history as the Thinkerman of football.

18

Leicester's Numbers

The miracle of Leicester will be recorded historically as one of the greatest moments in European football. Similar events have occurred, but it does not happen very often because the power of the teams vary; as years pass, the rich get richer, the powerful become more powerful, and the gap becomes larger. This inconceivable triumph of an underdog team against the best was an unexpected win beyond all expectations that touched everyone's heart. Above all, such an extraordinary feat leads one to reexamine the most common perception of all—that all that matters is money and in order for a team to win a trophy, they must have a huge capital investment.

The most popular cases where a team came out of nowhere, absolute underdogs that claimed the title in their country's championship, are recorded on the following chart.

Leicester's Numbers

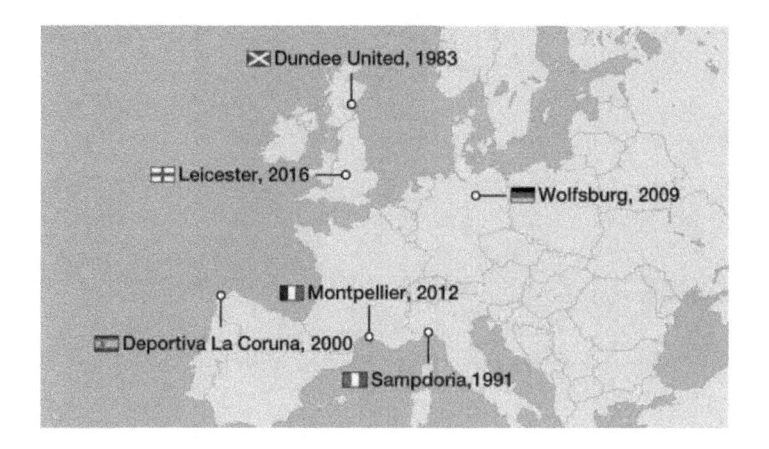

- Dundee United, 1983
- Leicester, 2016
- Wolfsburg, 2009
- Montpellier, 2012
- Deportiva La Coruna, 2000
- Sampdoria, 1991

Ranieri was known as the Tinkerman from his coaching days with Chelsea. The name was used to mock him for tinkering with the player line-ups during matches. The name was dumped when Leicester won the championship. He used the least amount of players than any other team in the competition and that's how the Foxes won the title.

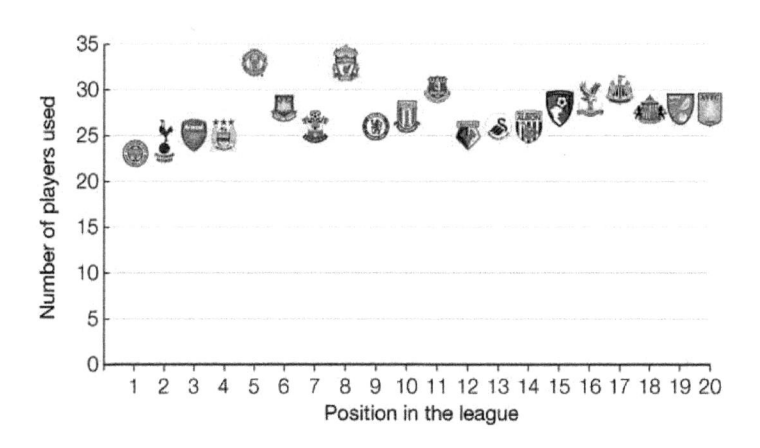

CLAUDIO RANIERI – T(H)INKERMAN

Leicester's stability during the 2015-2016 season against teams that were trying to catch them was impressive.

Many believed Ranieri's squad would not be able to last, especially after the Christmas holidays. As you will note on the season chart, no other team was really a threat to the Foxes after the second half of the Premier League 2015-2016. They never fell below sixth place, where they were for only a short time.

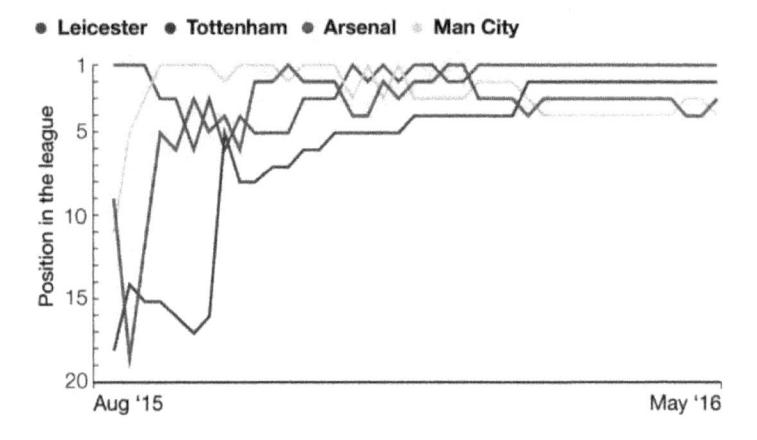

The fact that it was obvious early on that Leicester would become champion in England—mainly because the team just breezed right on through, but also for the consistency in their results—forced traditionally better teams to throw in the towel in 2015-2016.

The end result was that Ranieri's Leicester won the championship with fewer points than any other winner of recent years. They did not go over 80 points, unlike City, United, and Chelsea, which needed to go over 80 points in order to be crowned champions.

Leicester's Numbers

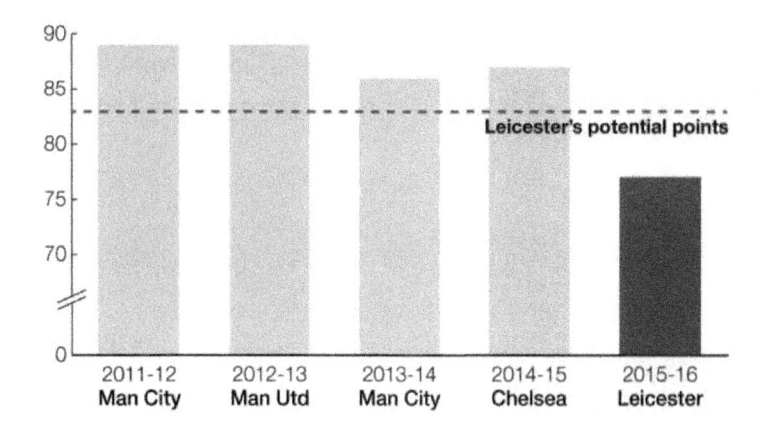

[Bar chart showing points: 2011-12 Man City ~89, 2012-13 Man Utd ~89, 2013-14 Man City ~86, 2014-15 Chelsea ~87, 2015-16 Leicester ~77, with Leicester's potential points marked around 82]

Great Britain's event of the year was undeniably the league title and the way it was won. Social media was taken by storm every time that Vardy scored. Twitter statistics are very impressive; there were over 3,000,000 posts on the day that the title win was officially announced. Vardy's goal against Sunderland on April 10 inspired 2,000,000 users to post about it.

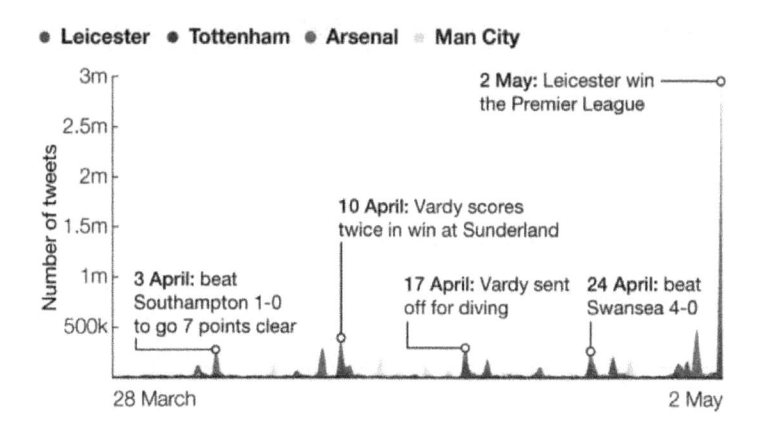

[Graph: Number of tweets — Leicester, Tottenham, Arsenal, Man City, from 28 March to 2 May]

- **3 April**: beat Southampton 1-0 to go 7 points clear
- **10 April**: Vardy scores twice in win at Sunderland
- **17 April**: Vardy sent off for diving
- **24 April**: beat Swansea 4-0
- **2 May**: Leicester win the Premier League

Leicester's most powerful weapons were none other than Jamie Vardy and Riyad Mahrez. In almost all the individual divisions they were able to make a difference and were the ones who changed the balance of Ranieri's team.

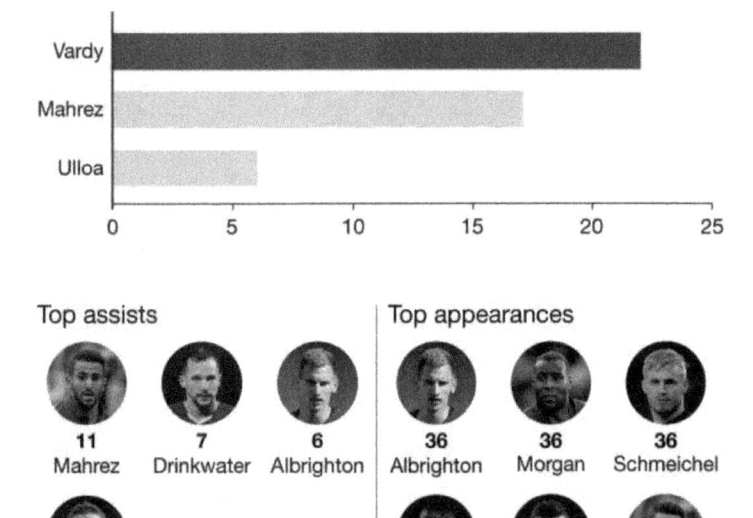

Player	Value
Vardy	~22
Mahrez	~17
Ulloa	~6

Top assists
- 11 Mahrez
- 7 Drinkwater
- 6 Albrighton
- 6 Vardy

Top appearances
- 36 Albrighton
- 36 Morgan
- 36 Schmeichel
- 35 Kante
- 35 Huth
- 35 Mahrez

Is it possible to buy success with money? Judging from the 2015-2016 season, the answer is no, you cannot buy success. For the first time in 25 years, the championship of England was not won by one of the traditional winning teams such as Arsenal, Chelsea, Manchester United, or Manchester City. At a time where television revenue was constantly increasing, with the last agreement being settled at over 5,000,000,000 GBP and the bigger share taken up by the more powerful, it seemed impossible that someone could break the chain of traditionally elite teams dominating it all. Leicester proved that in the end money does not have the leading role.

In 2015 Deloitte Sports Group Business published a report with the budgets of salaries that the teams in Britain have. The study has to do with all of the teams, mainly those that played in the Premier League after the 2013-2014 season, such as Leicester, Watford, and Bournemouth.

Even in this report we can see the gap between the Foxes and the other teams, especially the top ones.

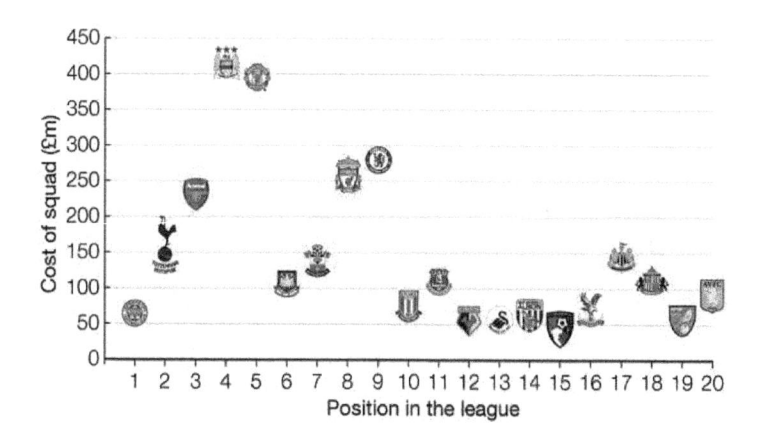

Stability was the main component of the team's success. The graph with the victories, defeats, and draws is indicative of the huge change that took place within a few months.

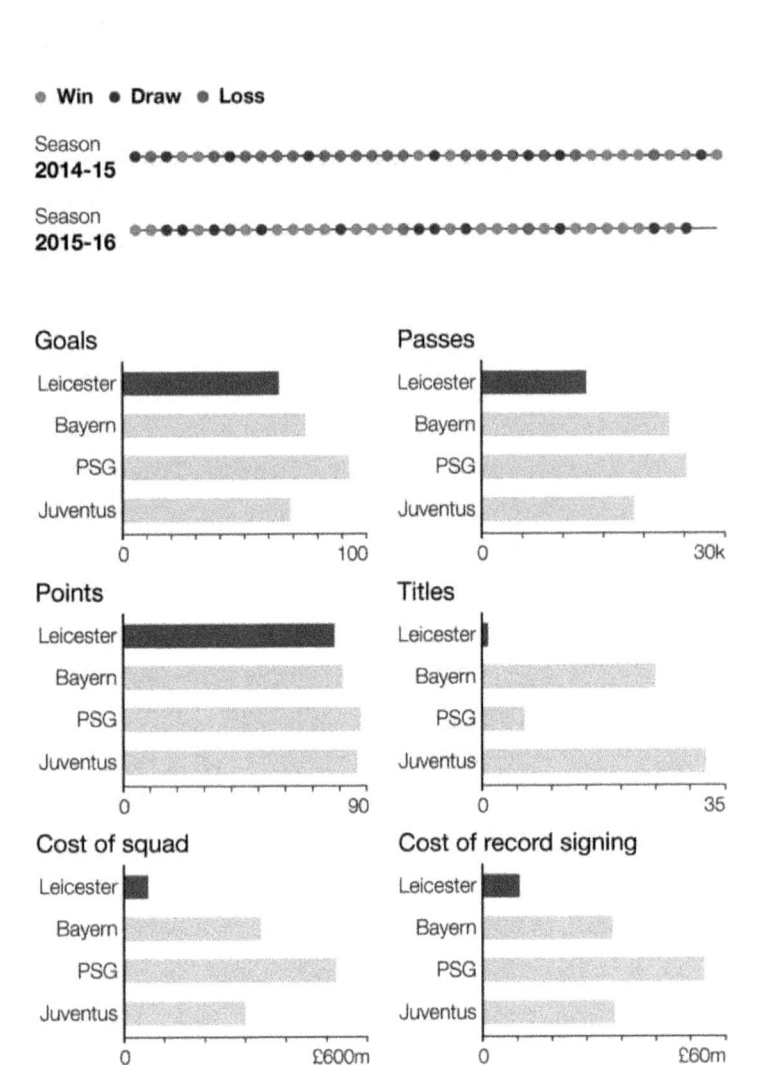

CLAUDIO RANIERI – T(H)INKERMAN

● Win ● Draw ● Loss

Season
2014-15

Season
2015-16

Goals
Leicester
Bayern
PSG
Juventus

0   100

Passes
Leicester
Bayern
PSG
Juventus

0   30k

Points
Leicester
Bayern
PSG
Juventus

0   90

Titles
Leicester
Bayern
PSG
Juventus

0   35

Cost of squad
Leicester
Bayern
PSG
Juventus

0   £600m

Cost of record signing
Leicester
Bayern
PSG
Juventus

0   £60m

19

The Ranieri Sausage

In the center of Leicester, on 99 Queens Road, the prominent sign on the butcher shop has been there for more than one hundred years; *W. Archer & Son* is printed in fancy letters, reminding everyone of the traditional shop where quality meat had always been sold.

Since the year 2000, the shop has been run by Sean Jeynes, a dedicated Leicester fan. Every Monday morning, during the 2015-2016 football season, there was always merrymaking at the butcher shop. Claudio Ranieri's players made the people happy with their performance, and the main topic of discussion was about the weekend football matches. The shop had a steady flow of customers and many of them were very popular members of the community. Leicester's Ulloa, like a true Latin American man, was a meat lover, and a customer of the shop.

When the 2015-2016 banger of a season began, many businesses that saw their sales declining due to the economic crisis wanted to identify with the Leicester football team to get into the festive commercial climate around and about the city.

When people are in high spirits, the creative portion of their minds can invent various successful gimmicks. There were many stores in the center of the city that changed their interior design to have a Leicester theme. They painted their walls in the team colors or decorated the walls with the Fox emblem to indirectly remind the customers of the strong name of the city's football team.

The butcher who worked at W. Archer & Son, Brian Gibbs, was charmed by Claudio Ranieri's personality and demeanor. The Italian had a way about him that captivated the hearts of everyone in the city. That is not necessarily the easiest thing in the world to do.

Leicester is a multicultural society with many immigrants and working-class people from various parts of the world. It is a cauldron full of traditions and customs. It is therefore practically impossible for someone or something to unite all these different cultures and philosophies of people living in the city. But Ranieri was able to bring everyone together through the city's football team.

One morning in February, the staff of the local butcher shop W. Archer & Son placed a chalkboard outside the shop on the pavement of 99 Queens Road with the Italian flag drawn on it and underneath it said, "Try our Ranieri Italian Sausage."

In the beginning, the customers did not really pay any mind to it and believed this to be a joke, something the owner, Sean Jeynes, usually did to entertain the customers. But whoever read the sign carefully, learned that the shop had a special edition sausage named after Ranieri. They used his name for a new handmade product to attract the customers and the sales skyrocketed. When the news of this traveled around the city that there was a butcher shop with a sausage named for Ranieri, many people went out of curiosity to buy some sausage and try it.

The Ranieri Sausage

So he helped the shop in his own special way. He was flattered by the gesture of the butcher shop to make his own sausage and name it Ranieri. Having worked in a butcher shop in Testaccio, he knew many secrets of the trade.

On Friday, April 1, 2016, on the eve of the game against Southampton, he was going to give the usual pre-game press conference at King Power. A surprise was waiting for him there. When he was speaking and analyzing the way the team would be playing in the match the next day, two men approached him holding a very big tray and interrupted the press conference.

They had come to serve him Ranieri sausages. Of course, being the master of social interaction, he enjoyed the humor of the situation and reached over and took a slice and tasted it.

After he swallowed the bit of sausage he said, "Thank you, I am honored, but too much garlic for me!"

Everyone in the room laughed hysterically.

The whole event, his comments, and amusing reactions, became world news. The media around the world, the Internet, newspapers, and television, everyone was talking about the Ranieri sausage.

The local butcher shop, W. Archer & Son, that invented the Ranieri Sausage became known around the world by that one sentence that Claudio spoke. Everyone wanted to know what else the sausage had in it and if there really was too much garlic.

The customers increased because everyone ran to the shop looking for a taste. The shop's financial turnover increased as well. He had helped a local butcher shop in the middle of the city with his reaction to the whole situation without even realizing it. There was nothing in it for him financially, only personal amusement and honor.

Since then, the city has had many visitors seeking the W. Archer & Son butcher shop in order to pop in and buy some Ranieri sausage, which has become a must for anyone going through Leicester.

20

The Legend of King Richard III and the Supernatural Title Win

The city of Leicester is one of the most ethnically diverse cities in the UK.

The east region of the Midlands spans the counties of Leicestershire, Derbyshire, Northamptonshire, Nottinghamshirer, Rutland, and Lincolnshire. Leicester is 100 miles north of London; you can take the train and within an hour and ten minutes you can be at the part of the city that is mainly for students.

The 330,000 residents of Leicester, and those from surrounding areas, had more of a nostalgic relationship with football because they always believed they would never be able to have the glory and glamor that the London teams do.

Leicester was best known for its hosiery factories, which flourished around the 19th century, and for its working class population.

Based on the history of English football, the team's success is truly miraculous. We can find proof of this if we look at the statistics from the start of the Premier League in 1992, where we will notice that only five teams have managed to win the league: Manchester United has won thirteen times, Chelsea four, Arsenal three, Manchester City twice, and Blackburn once. Up until Leicester's win, these were the only teams that managed to reach the top of the British League.

The English league is hard and rough, but unique and exciting, and it gains more fans around the globe as time goes on, because of its originality.

The most typical trait of this is the fact that from 1999 to 2010 only two teams, Arsenal and Manchester United, finished in the top four of all eleven championships. Chelsea and Liverpool finished in the top four in eight of those eleven seasons.

Traditional clubs with very long histories, many fans, and enormous investments reached the top and went after the title every season. It is always the same teams. You can count them on the fingers of one hand. They are far above the other teams and are able to compete with legendary teams from all over Europe, on all levels.

This further demonstrates the magnitude of Ranieri and his squad's success. Such a thing is incredible to achieve. The underdog of practically every season shoots to the top and stays there for the entire duration of the season in one of the most difficult leagues of the world.

It seemed unreal that Leicester—a team that had just been promoted only two years earlier and had been on the brink of relegation the previous season—would be able to break the record of these top four teams, which are traditionally the big favorites, and also win the championship. For someone who is a fan of English football and knows much about it, it was simply improbable and incredible, and would only occur if some supernatural force were behind it.

The question that everyone tried to answer was how Ranieri and the team did it with all the odds completely against them. It was out of the question if one were to think about how the history of English football has progressed through time.

People who occasionally love a mystery believe that an explanation for these phenomena can be found in the realms of the metaphysical, since it's something that rarely happens in the physical world. Speaking about such fantasies can create an atmosphere of mass hysteria, or they can become legends, even if they do not have a trace of plausibility. But they do give a special magical tinge to things and make one wonder.

So then, what really happened for Ranieri and his squad? No one will be able to determine exactly what force was with the team, no matter how many metaphysical, fantastical, or legendary vibes the whole happening may have. It will remain a mystery.

When Leicester won the title, many people became superstitious or at least they reached the point where you would think they were superstitious. You would even think that Claudio Ranieri himself was superstitious judging by certain little rituals he had before and after every match. Things that he does for luck. All one has to do is study certain habits of his to come to this conclusion.

His signature blue striped tie, which he wore many times under his coat or team jacket, had some sort of mystical quality. It gave element to the myth and superstition. Many still believe today that this was what helped him get to the championship.

His mobile phone and people ringing him again and again certainly played a part, for anyone who would like to give a metaphysical dimension to the success. From January 2016, I would always send a congratulatory message to Claudio's mobile phone. I later learned that many of his friends, old colleagues, and people he met through the years of his football career did exactly the same thing.

My message to him contained the same magic word every time. For positive energy. For luck. Since it worked the first time, I repeated it every time.

Dear Claudio would always respond a little while later in his own special way, with just one very pleasant word. He did the same for everyone.

During the days of the championship, the messages of support had a dose of anticipation in them because the dream seemed to be nigh. He was always polite and generous when replying with the same one-worded magic message. It was his lucky charm. Apparently, I was not the only who wanted to send my positive energy in this habitual way.

Reaching the end of the journey, this ritual did not change. When I met him, I reminded him of this and he laughed.

Today, I see it in a more casual light because the messages are one of his good luck habits. Answering to everyone, always in a specific way, and to everyone separately, not in a group message. Yes, it was always his way before and after something big and important was to occur.

Even though it seemed he thought and acted intuitively, you can see by what he says in his public statements—his actions revealed this—that in the end he was more a rationalist, as we saw the year that Leicester won the title.

Success was derived from his good choices, both during daily training when preparing the team, and during critical moments where he needed to make significant alterations. Yes, he became Tinkerman when he needed to shift the tactics around during a match. He put his philosophy in motion when he needed to take the pressure off of his players during a difficult time in the championship, when he could feel the breath of the pursuers on his back.

In the city, of course, they are living their own fairy tale, and like all fairy tales, this one has its adventures. Many people are very sure it is a miracle and that the resurrection of the team can be attributed to the events I write about below.

Until recently, the fate of King Richard the III's body following his death at the Battle of Bosworth Field remained an unsolved mystery over which generations of archeologists and historians of Great Britain pondered greatly. This mystery was solved in September of 2012 when archeologists from the University of Leicester discovered the remains of the king almost intact under a car lot. For many people this was a sign from the universe that meant the fate of the city—and their football team—would be altered.

The anthropological and genetic tests that were carried out to confirm the identity of the remains took years. The discovery of the king's tomb was a very big deal. When the body was finally identified, it marked the answer to the burning question, and ended a mystery that existed for hundreds of years. It was a happy end. A happy end that was spiritually linked with all that followed.

After the identity of King Richard was confirmed, a proper reburial was held for him at the Leicester Cathedral in March 2015, and he was laid to rest with full honors. The ceremony was solemn, as it should be for a king. The Archbishop of Canterbury was present and the ceremony was broadcast live on television. During the ceremony, actor Benedict Cumberbatch, a distant relative of King Richard III, recited a poem. It was the event of the year.

That is, until the next emotional event took place.

When all this was taking place, the team was in last place of the Premier League and no one expected the bizarre title win, not even in their wildest dreams. In some ways Leicester was the only team which was the standard favorite to be relegated. But after the tomb was found, the Foxes won seven out of the last nine matches of the season. This was not only a surprise, it was a miracle that coincided with what the city was experiencing. With those seven wins, the team remained in the Premier League.

Many already strongly believed that some paranormal activity affected the team. This belief was adopted by almost the entire city after King Richard's bones were discovered. Many read into it and believed the miraculous leap to the top was because the king showered them with positive energy. Others were skeptical and considered the whole story to be just an eerie coincidence.

The fact that Leicester won the title, the fact that they remained on top for most of the season, in one of the strongest leagues in the world, the fact that they lost only four matches the whole season, and the fact that they won the Premier League is a miracle within itself, regardless of anything else.

The Legend of King Richard III and the Supernatural Title Win

It is difficult to make an analysis in football in order to conclude what the deciding factor was for Leicester's outstanding achievement. There are many reasons, mainly the team's competitive ability and outstanding technique, but the metaphysical aspect that is discussed always excites the sports fans.

Leicester was not even in the Premier League two years before they won the title, and relegation was hot on their heels. Seven years before they won the title, they were in the third division of England, and if someone had bet on it, they would never have guessed that the underdog would become a superstar one day.

In some cases, it often happens that someone will suddenly come along with a lot of money and heave the traditional teams with a long history to the top. In other cases, large companies that operate in sectors such as energy and technology find a good channel through football teams and come to them with the clear objective of taking advantage of the circumstances and reaping the benefits. Perhaps when a crazy businessman makes his investment to display or promote his business in this way, it can be a good opportunity to find funds.

When Claudio first joined Leicester and heard about the story of King Richard the III and the way the city's luck changed after the discovery, he did not miss the chance to go to the museum and learn about it in detail.

He often motivates his players by telling them they have an obligation towards the city's king to overcome their limits. Everyone laughs uncontrollably whenever he says such things. But the legend of the king and his positive energy followed them in the 2015-2016 season.

Yes, it happens to be a very nice story that stimulates the residents' imaginations, but reality and realism have prevailed.

The team had a goal and they worked for it. Leicester had a solid foundation and that is where their brilliant Italian coach came in with his own way of building onto it. Everything else that took place occurred because nature took its course.

21

Claudio's Magic Wand

"You know a winning team by the way they celebrate together. That's how you know if everyone is committed to a common goal. You can see in the way they defend. Just like in war, if you are willing to fall for the man next to you, you can always achieve anything."

If the legendary Bob Paisley were alive to see Ranieri's achievements with his players, his would surely be misty-eyed. His words were certainly applied many years later during Leicester's mythical course, which led to their pot of gold in England the 2015-2016 season.

Maybe what changed the situation and brought Ranieri to the top was their start together.

There are world views about football, which may be considered obligatory preconditions for the way a coach works with a team. Many times these views come into contrast with already existing circumstances, and sometimes they conflict with one's technical approach to the sport. In order for him to work with Leicester, he had to change his own existing world view about the sport.

With all the teams he had previously worked with, he was the boss and had the last say in everything, from beginning to end. For instance, when the proposal was made for him to go to Athens and manage the national team of Greece, it was left in his hands to completely revamp the team and change the existing image.

The difference in his working with Leicester was that from the very first day, he was also working with the staff of the team, which was there at the time Nigel Pearson was coaching. In June of 2015, when Claudio was appointed, he found himself in front of something entirely different than what he was used to in his coaching career.

The precondition to work with Leicester was that he must accept the same staff that was previously working with Pearson. He would have to cooperate and work with people he did not know but who were trusted by the club. This was something new for him and he had to learn to live with it, and manage as best he could, because he knew all too well that in order to achieve results quickly, he would have to cooperate with people he basically did not previously know existed.

Therefore, he was forced to accept the professional skills of people that he did not know. Two basic qualities were needed in order for the collaboration to succeed: trust and cooperation. For trust to be built, the results of the team and time would play a major role. In football everything is judged by the results and hard work is rewarded when you succeed. As far as cooperation was concerned, he had shown the way he worked with people when he was the coach of other teams, even the ones that did not do well. Nobody ever accused him of having a character flaw or of displaying bad behavior.

In the global football scene, in all divisions, the precondition is the coach must be in complete control. When he heard that a precondition with Leicester was to not change anyone from the team, he was ready to do just that. He knew better than anyone that you will succeed when you are cooperative. The best chef in the world can create and get Michelin stars for his cuisine, but he cannot prepare his specialties by himself; but if one of his assistants adds more salt than is needed, it might ruin the chef's career.

This is exactly what he understood perfectly well in July of 2015, when he sat down to talk to Leicester's crew. The sports science team of the club was well known for its good collaboration over the last few years. Many times, though, it can be unfair to some wonderful experts, because their work is judged based on the way the players perform on the pitch.

It is something unfair in football: if the ball misses the net by half a meter, the science sports team is at fault, but if it goes half a meter in, the sports science team is wonderful.

It is quite difficult for the doctors, physiotherapists, trainers, nutritionists, and coaches to be synchronized so that they can fit together as a subset, which must run like clockwork for the team. At the beginning, Ranieri was forced to pay more attention to how the staff operated, to guide them and initiate them to his own training program. He also had to listen and trust their judgment as well.

There are various standard things in a coach's job that cannot be changed, and there are some directives that the big clubs follow. Many times the main element of success is neither knowledge nor the diplomas that one carries. Especially in clubs that have expensive star players, what makes a coach special is his ability to keep balance within the team. There have been many cases where the star players have a more important status than that of the manager himself.

They have bigger contracts and can be the ones running the show. Character and diplomacy and managing the moment is what makes a successful tactician. Throughout his career he was perceptive with all of his players and communicated with them pragmatically by approaching them with thoughtfulness and giving them a lot of himself, while keeping the role of coach and player separate.

Many times his tactics from team to team did not differ, but were not effective in all the clubs he worked as shown in the results they produced. Other times, the tactics he used were not compatible with the players' characters. There are quite a few examples of this from his time on the bench of the Greek national team. When Ranieri was coaching them, his tactics were foreign to the players, but they also did not want to use his system, even if it was convenient for them, because their biorhythms were programmed differently and they had a particular way of working.

The Greek national team implemented a system, which was largely based on absolute idleness on the eve of the matches, and decompression before a match. On the day of the match, they would wake up late in the morning and eat a big breakfast, without restrictions. Then later on, they could enjoy their coffee until lunchtime and after that a siesta was necessary. A few hours before leaving the hotel, they would have a quick snack and immediately board the bus for the stadium, completely rested.

When Ranieri started working with them, some things in their schedule changed. The players were required to wake up early and on the day of the match they could relax with low-intensity exercises or with resistance exercises for a shorter duration. They were used to other patterns and a different way of preparation on the day of the match. They were accustomed to a totally different schedule for years and that needed to change.

Nobody can say for sure what the suitable methods are and how a coach and the players can be evaluated by them. Ranieri used the same method with Leicester and was successful, but a year earlier with the Greek team the same thing was a complete failure. This brings us to the question of whether he should adjust himself to what the players are used to or if the players should adjust themselves to his methods.

The magical year that Leicester conquered the Premier League, there were some unsung heroes working behind the scenes. Each one of them wrote their own history when their time came.

CLAUDIO RANIERI – T(H)INKERMAN

Claudio's Jet Fighters

Leicester player	Position	Appearances	Time (min)	Total distance (km)	Average distance per 90 minutes (km)
Leonardo Ulloa	Forward	22	767	93.43	10.96
Marc Albrighton	Midfielder	30	2476	300.62	10.92
Shinji Okazaki	Forward	28	1661	201.45	10.91
Andy King	Midfielder	21	1035	124.32	10.82
N'Golo Kanté	Midfielder	29	2479	295.87	10.74
Riyad Mahrez	Midfielder	29	2496	289.39	10.43
Daniel Rinkwater	Midfielder	28	2580	297.39	10.37
Nathan Dyer	Midfielder	12	291	32.74	10.10
Christian Fuchs	Defender	24	2139	231.75	9.74
Ritchie De Laet	Defender	12	716	77.27	9.7
Jamie Vardy	Forward	30	2822	299.9	9.56
Jeffrey Schlupp	Midfielder	18	1223	128.37	9.44
Danny Simpson	Defender	22	2018	209.26	9.33
Robert Huth	Defender	29	2817	263.41	8.41
Wes Morgan	Defender	30	2908	263.71	8.16

Leicester moving to the top of the charts in the 2015-2016 season was the main topic of discussion for many weeks, not only for British media, but worldwide as well.

When champion Chelsea was struggling to keep up, Ranieri's Leicester was at the top of the standings. The most prominent move the Italian made was his tactics with Vardy. On top teams, the most aggressive player always works as a barometer for the way the team operates. If the striker succeeds in measuring his choices on the pitch and follows through, then the team will automatically run like clockwork.

He gave him freedom on the pitch and told him to use all of the space, to play freely in the second half when they did not have possession of the ball, and to strike whenever possible and wherever his resources were needed. This gave freedom to strike in the larger areas. Most players have a certain area they play in, but not Vardy. Being the team barometer, he was weatherproof.

He knew well that if he were to use Vardy only on the left or the right shoulder, he would confine him. He would not be able to get 100% of his capabilities, so this way he was in every play or else he was forced to resort to the 4-3-3 defense formation. On the other hand, if he were to put him on top of the attack, Jamie would have to face the problem by himself among the stoppers that most teams have.

Ranieri wanted Vardy to move about freely using the 4-2-2 formation, partnering with Okazaki. Many times Ulloa would play Okazaki's role, gathering up any lost balls and leaving the plays to Vardy, who would be in the right place at the right time. When Claudio decided to close spaces off, he would go to a 4-5-1 formation. He knew well that he had his jet fighter running enough for two or three players, many times resulting in his team outnumbering the opponents.

He would unleash Vardy and allow him to run toward the goal by himself and the rest of the team would masterfully close off all the areas. With his lightning speed and astounding stamina, Jamie ran all over the pitch nonstop during every match. At any time he could outrun the opposite defense and come face to face with the goalposts. He is an impressive scorer and he rarely makes a mistake when an opportunity arises to score. The way he plays the game is such that the opponent can never predict where he will go.

With Leicester Ranieri usually employs the old classic 4-4-2 formation in most of the matches, with players on the line and without a clear attacking midfielder. This tactic was revolutionary for the English league. It allowed for the full utilization of the men he had on the wings rather than the center.

Mahrez and Albrighton were two of the best during the season that Leicester won the championship. When Nigel Pearson was coach of Leicester, Riyad Mahrez did not have a particular position. But when Ranieri became coach, he allowed for Mahrez's liftoff by giving him a role in the matches. Claudio believed in the ability of players who were considered losers. Albrighton was essentially established as a left winger and was a hard-working runner on the wings. Leicester played with real wingers and surprised the other teams that took some time to realize the strategy Leicester was using.

You will find Mahrez or Albrighton on almost every list of the top scorers, assisters, dribblers, and the players that covered the most kilometers on the pitch. They were two of the keys to Leicester winning the Premier League.

Cambiasso rejecting his contract extension shocked the club when the Argentinean announced that he would continue his career in Greece to play for the Olympiacos team. The previous year had been excellent for Cambiasso. Given his experience, many felt that his retirement from Leicester was a huge loss because he could contribute effectively to Leicester's middle line. Nigel Pearson had supported the whole defense operation with the majority of it being covered by Cambiasso.

Ranieri, on the other hand, knowing the statistics well, used the colpo grosso strategy and put two men in midfield and two jet fighters on the wings. One of them was N'Golo Kanté, a player that can run with the power of two or even three men on the pitch.

He put Danny Drinkwater alongside them in the lineup, giving him more appearances than he previously had. He is an amazing defensive midfielder, who is all over the pitch. He was entirely Ranieri's discovery as he believed in his ability and put him in. He channeled this spirit and passion of having faith in victory to the players. He believed in the players and gave them a chance by supporting them, and they in turn gave the best of themselves. Those who use the positive energy he generated have vindicated him much more than he could ever have wished for. A message that everyone can follow in their lives comes from the way the Leicester players were managed.

The result? Champions of the Premier League.

22

Hello, Sharks, Welcome to the Funeral

Shortly after the worst moment of Ranieri's career—the defeat of the Greek national team by the Faroe Islands—I was waiting for him for a flash interview, so he could make a statement for our state-owned television station. I knew that it was his swan song for Greece and, obviously, he knew as well. The mood was a little awkward. Claudio, however, appeared at ease and particularly calm. He knew all too well what had taken place. The damage had already been done so there was nothing he could say that would make a difference. There was no sense in his trying to justify the unjustifiable. He had told me before the match that the players did not need a coach to beat Faroe. The question at that moment that mattered was if he would remain with the Greek national team.

"Mr. Ranieri, twenty-four players will not be leaving the team, are you thinking about leaving?"

Someone from the public relations crew of the team—there were many at the time—who was standing a few meters away, went pale and grimaced. You would think I had asked him the question and not Ranieri. I have seen these looks many times before in my career. People who confuse their own roles with that of the protagonist. In this case, Ranieri was the protagonist.

Before the question could be interpreted into Italian, he had understood it, and he smiled. He was quite calm and especially experienced. He had been asked similar questions before. He looked at me and answered very naturally.

"If someone is responsible and that someone is me, then maybe I will."

He did not hide, he was not afraid, and he did not keep what he felt to himself. A few hours later he resigned from the national team of Greece, although some people said that they forced him to resign because of the issue with the compensation payment.

Ranieri's relationship with the reporters has always been very civil, but he has received very harsh criticism quite a few times by some of them. Sometimes it was very unfair, but he was always respectable and also respected a reporter's job.

Before Chelsea's second match of the Champions League with Monaco, a few days after the first semifinal in London, when he was on Chelsea's bench, he said to the reporters at a press conference, "Hello, my sharks, welcome to the funeral."

The sharks were waiting for blood and Claudio had set the tone.

When I arrived in Leicester to see him a few weeks before he celebrated the championship win at King Power, the press box was packed as if the World Cup and Olympic Games were going on simultaneously. Journalists from around the world had traveled to come and record the team's feat. In order to get authorization to cover a football match, you need to apply about six weeks in advance; I had some volunteers who put various obstacles out for me, so that I would not be able to get an interview. Claudio always respected my work and did whatever he could to help me do my job. He did not hold a grudge against me for everything he had gone through in Greece and the humiliating way he was treated.

More than two hundred requests had been made to the press office for interviews with their coach. It was a tremendous honor when, for the next game against Newcastle, I passed through the door of the training grounds to talk with Claudio Ranieri, who at the time was everyone's favorite to win for the title.

He was now the most sought-after person to meet and interview. He was something along the lines of meeting Barack Obama or Vladimir Putin. Something happened that illustrates perfectly what it means to manage even to see Ranieri, let alone interview him.

At the gates of the training grounds, there were photographers scattered, waiting to get a picture of Vardy and the other Leicester players. They were mainly focused on Vardy because a few days earlier he bought a new Bentley in the team colors, and a picture of him in the driver's seat was handsomely paid for by the British tabloids. There were many Japanese reporters there, watching and recording the team's progress every day. They were there to cover Leicester, but also to interview Okazaki. They gave live reports and were perfectly adapted to the climate and atmosphere.

Giuseppe is a great reporter of state-owned Italian television. He managed to stop me before entering the main gate of the training grounds. A guard had blown the whistle on me and told him that Claudio will be speaking to a Greek journalist. Giuseppe was perfectly polite when he spoke to me.

"Good morning, I see you have a camera there. Will you be interviewing Ranieri?" he asked.

"Yes, he will be interviewed for the Greek state-owned network," I replied.

His eyes grew in surprise, because he thought it was rather odd that Ranieri would be giving an exclusive interview to a Greek reporter from the country that had upset him. Giuseppe had been waiting there for two months for only a statement from his compatriot, and he hadn't been successful.

He was monitoring the preparations before the game as a correspondent, but his attention was mainly focused on Claudio's work.

He offered me a lot of money not to go into the training grounds and to cancel my interview so that he could take my place and finally get his own interview. I literally laughed out loud. I automatically recalled the years at the stadiums, where I had stood out in the rain and cold, chasing after exclusive interviews. The irony! I was going to Leicester with a borrowed camera and the Italian was offering me a fortune to take my place for his own exclusive interview with Ranieri.

You can taste how sweet the moral of this story is. No matter how many obstacles are put in your path, no matter how hard they try to stop you with nasty means, in the end you will win if you stay focused on your goal. Ranieri won and became king just like that, by believing in his goal. I smiled politely and thanked my fellow reporter.

Within thirty minutes the camera had recorded Claudio sending a message to the Greek sports fans among other things. A few days later, the interview was the main topic on a BBC program with Thierry Henry. The evening news of the station I work for in Greece never even played a minute segment of our interview after it was aired on the program Athletic Sunday. A very sad work environment.

The year before Ranieri arrived, Leicester had a fantastic second round in the English championship and literally saved the day at the last minute. Nigel Pearson had received all the glory and no one, not even as a fantasy, could ever have believed that he would be leaving Leicester.

Towards the end of the championship, a few weeks before the final, while the Foxes were on their way to reaching the goal of remaining in the Premier League, a defeat by Chelsea turned everything upside down. Pearson, for no apparent reason, lost his temper at the press conference after the match, when a journalist asked a follow-up question. He retorted:

"If you don't know the answer to that question, then I think you're an ostrich. Your head must be in the sand. Is your head in the sand? I think you are either being very silly or you're being absolutely stupid."

He went on to say it was impossible to speak to the press about serious issues because they have no idea about team management. After that came a media circus and, of course, as in any country, in Britain the press would not let it go.

A trip to Bangkok would be Pearson's last ride with Leicester. In order for those who knew nothing about team management (i.e., reporters) to punish him, they decided to disclose everything that happened on that trip to Bangkok at the end of the 2014-2015 season. The owner of the team comes from Thailand.

A newspaper got a hold of a video showing three Leicester players having a party with Thai prostitutes. Not only that, the players—having consumed alcohol—were spewing racial slurs about the girls and their country. The video was posted on the internet and it caused a pandemonium. The sharks ate Pearson alive. The road to Leicester had opened for Claudio Ranieri. Pearson will certainly think twice about insulting or belittling anyone again, especially a reporter.

The Italian reporters had long since expressed their desire to see him on the bench of the Italian national team. Even Carlo Tavecchio, the president of the Italian Football Federation, during an award ceremony for Italian coaches, openly told Ranieri, the winner of the Premier League, that he wished he would go to Squadra Azzurra's bench. On the whole, the Italian journalists proclaimed him to be the best coach and the ball was in his court to decide. The nightmare, however, of the Greek national team did not leave him any margin whatsoever to even think about it.

Tavecchio also said that he thought that after the Premier League, Ranieri would try for a World Cup.

"I hope that Claudio will win a World cup with Italy. That would be the best. I'm speaking in an abstract way, of course, and not necessarily about the next World Cup. Claudio is still young and has a lot of time ahead to train.

"Have we thought about him as a replacement for Conte? That is something you will have to ask Claudio himself if he will think about it. We're thinking about a lot of different things right now. It is an honor for Italy that a coach from our country won the Premier League title. Competition, dedication, and a deep sense of duty are all features that are recognized in Ranieri."

Ranieri was quite definite in his reply because in this instance, the saying once bitten, twice shy applies.

"The Italian bench? For me an international job is a closed chapter. I was already burned in Greece."

He had learned his lesson painfully. Claudio knew that the last thing that he would be doing would be to coach an international team again.

23

How Things Change

By winning the title with Leicester, Ranieri clearly showed that a coach—or better yet, a man—can change. He can be transformed even at 64 years old. He remains the same person, but he corrects his mistakes. He can adapt, assimilate, and learn from the past to interpret the present, he can understand and be understood, he can mature professionally.

Going through older newspaper publications, one notices that this kind man—maybe more than necessary—was both glorified and chewed apart. Never in the history of world press has a man been scoffed at and glorified within a year and a half.

It is unbelievable the way the public opinion shifted and Claudio changed from an ugly duckling into a swan based on the publications that circulated. When he first started out, most Greek newspapers had written about him respectfully without a lot of fanfare. There was some hesitation because the Greek national team's appearance in the Mundial did not leave a lot of room for it to continue, no matter who sat on the bench after Fernando Santos.

Claudio's life over the last two years has been a mixture of cold and hot. The way the newspapers treated him in his worst and best moments of his career was quite illustrative. The contrast of emotions was intense, but he endured it all with nerves of steel. He was experienced and had gone through several stormy seas earlier in his life, but also in his career.

In recent years, the press in Greece had been going through a crisis and it is something that is reflected in the newspapers that circulate. News is of secondary importance and in order for the sports pages to survive they have to identify with the behavior of the teams in order to gain readers.

After the dramatic struggle with the Faroe Islands, which marked the termination of his contract with the national team of Greece with Ranieri, newspapers lashed out at the Italian coach, but also against the whole system of the Hellenic Football Federation. The press was waiting for the failure for some time.

Newspaper *SportDay* printed a picture of the EPO president, Giorgos Sarris, speaking with Ranieri. The aggressive headline read, *"Yes, you've ruined us."*

GOAL newspaper was telling Claudio Ranieri resign on his own. From the beginning of his stint with the Greek national team, they criticized almost all of his choices harshly.

CLAUDIO RANIERI – T(H)INKERMAN

How Things Change

Greek newspaper *FOS* spoke of national humiliation and called the defeat by Faroe the "Titanic" of the century.

But life goes around in circles and after bombing out, Ranieri rose to glory within a year and a half. The pages in British newspapers the day after the title win were historical. Such stories of miracles rarely occur. Leicester winning the Premier League was such a miracle. The headlines of the newspapers were wildly enthusiastic and reflected the euphoric atmosphere in Britain.

CLAUDIO RANIERI – T(H)INKERMAN

How Things Change

CLAUDIO RANIERI – T(H)INKERMAN

How Things Change

CLAUDIO RANIERI – T(H)INKERMAN

How Things Change

THE TIMES

Blair and Bill Clinton join forces in campaign against Brexit

PM plans new laws to stop Muslim extremists

Cameron reasserts authority in Queen's Speech

Fairytale finish for champions Leicester

CLAUDIO RANIERI – T(H)INKERMAN

How Things Change

Around the world, Leicester's accomplishment, and especially Claudio Ranieri's, created a panic in the media all over the world. For several days, newspapers were filling the headlines in tribute to Leicester City. His compatriots had one more reason to dedicate their headlines to this as they were so proud of Leicester's miraculous win. Never in the history of football has any other story had this much coverage by the press. It was one of the greatest victories in the history of football. The Italian newspaper *Corriere della Sera* hailed Ranieri as King Claudio.

How Things Change

The *Gazzeta dello Sport* had the most remarkable headline with Claudio as the Roman emperor Claudius. The newspaper broke every sales record that day.

171

The headline of the newspaper *TuttoSport* also referred to Ranieri as King of England.

How Things Change

Spain's newspaper *Marca* wittily played with words by integrating the Spanish word *olé* into the team's name along with a picture of Ranieri rejoicing.

The *AS* wrote that Leicester becoming champion was the miracle of the century.

How Things Change

In Portugal, newspaper *ABOLA* had a picture of Leicester fans celebrating and the caption read "Leicester is champion."

175

CLAUDIO RANIERI – T(H)INKERMAN

Spanish newspaper *El Mundo Deportivo* filled their front page with Leicester's miracle and had a picture of Vardy at home with his teammates celebrating their victory.

How Things Change

The French newspaper L'Equipe wrote their title in English in honor of Leicester's smashing win.

24

Leicester's Market Value

The football stock market is astonishingly stimulating. A team's purchasing power is almost always linked to the resale value their commercial products may have. In this case that means the players. If a goal is scored, if a title is won, that can mean an increase in value of the player's share.

There are some stories that are like fairytales about the value increase of a player happening within a very short time. This usually stems from the player's personal performance. It concerns the offence players mostly because they have the ability to score and change their performance image more quickly. The value of a midfielder can depend on his overall on-field performance, but that can also depend on the team as a whole.

In Italy's 1990 Mundial, when Toto Schillaci appeared, nobody could believe that a month later his market value would sky rocket, making his contract worth 50 times more. This happened because the national team of Italy managed to reach the semifinals and Schillaci scored in every match. He was a star player and it took just one month for everything to change for him, although the continuation did not follow accordingly.

There are many other examples of players whose values increased dramatically because of a fantastic goal or an appearance in a big match. Leicester's title win, however, has no precedent in the world of football history. The resale value of all the players shot up compared to the money that had been paid to acquire them. Ranieri had a hand in this, and was able to get the best of them by using everything in his bag of tricks.

Leicester, with its 132-year history, won the title and the total value of the players who played the most minutes amounted to approximately 155,000,000 GBP. This is an honest to goodness blastoff, particularly in cases of players that were acquired when they were free.

The most outstanding case was that of Kasper Schmeichel for whom no money was paid to any team and only the money of his contract and salary were covered in the summer of 2011.

Today Schmeichel's market value is at approximately 12,000,000 GBP and one can consider that at 29 years of age his added value and share made such an explosion that it will be difficult to find him in the world football stock market again.

Danny Simpson played right-back for the Queens Park Rangers and in 2014 Leicester acquired him by paying 2,000,000 GBP. Simpson's market value increased to 5,000,000 GBP when Leicester won the title.

In the summer of 2015, when Schalke decided to let the Austrian Christian Fuchs go after four years of his playing for them, no one from the German team could have imagined how things would turn around for him. Fuchs ventured out to find a team on his own and knocked on many doors before he was accepted to Ranieri's Leicester. Exactly one year later, his market value increased from nil to 6,000,000 GBP.

Huth came to Leicester when he was 30 years old on loan from Stoke. In 2015, the Foxes—after prompting from Ranieri, who saw Huth as a defensive boulder for the team he wanted to build— paid 3,000,000 pounds to acquire him. A year later, if any team wants to knock on Leicester's door and ask for Huth, they will have to pay double that and more, around 7,000,000 GBP.

They said he was big and clumsy and no one really paid any attention to him at the beginning of his career. Wes Morgan is now the classic example of added value given to a Leicester player after the title win. Nottingham Forest sold him to Leicester in 2012, and 1,000,000 GBP was enough to dress him in the blue jersey. Five years later, his value is constantly rising. In the summer, Leicester was asked how much Morgan could be sold for and the answer was that he is worth approximately 10,000,000 GBP.

Marc Albrighton is a capable, conscientious winger who wore Aston Villa's jersey for five years and revealed several positive qualities that have made him an important player. But he was never a first-line player and he was released in 2014. He also ventured out on his own seeking refuge and was taken in by Leicester. Today if a team wants him to join them, they will have to pay more than 7,000,000 GBP.

The story of N'golo Kante shall be written in golden letters in the football bible. In the summer of 2015, Leicester paid

6,000,000 GBP to acquire Kante, and one year later they received 25,000,000 GBP from Chelsea. It was the ultimate deal. There was no other like it.

A player who rose alongside the team with his appearances on the British pitches catapulted his value into stupendous heights compared to the amount spent by the Foxes to acquire him.

Every summer, for the last five years, Manchester United would tell Danny Drinkwater that he should play on loan. He had grown tired of hearing this and realized that his career could not have the outcome he had dreamed about. United would not put their trust in him as a field player, so he would constantly hit the road for other teams. After four straight years of loans, Leicester decided to take the risk and paid 1,000,000 to acquire him. During the 2015-2016 season, Danny played for the national team of England. His market value is now 12,000,000 GBP and within one season he became one of the most important players in the Premier League.

I have written a separate chapter about Riyad Mahrez. Over the course of two years, Mahrez went from being valued at 350,000 GBP to being valued at 30,000,000 GBP. At 25 years old, he is one of the top players of the old continent.

The Fleetwood players' minds are on pubs and trying to find ways to make daily wages. Jamie Vardy's life had been anything but a dream the last few years.

Leicester paid amateur Fleetwood 1,000,000 GBP and now Vardy is valued at approximately 40,000,000 GBP. He and Mahrez are the legends of the Premier League.

CLAUDIO RANIERI – T(H)INKERMAN

The same goes for Okazaki from Japan, who introduced Leicester to the Far East. The best Japanese football player went to King Power from Mainz for about 7,000,000 GBP and today he is valued at over 16,000,000 GBP.

Claudio was able to get the ultimate quality out of each player. He instilled the spirit and psychology in them, putting them in a positive frame of mind that success was just around the corner. In football, a player's performance cannot change so dramatically in a very short period of time. A player cannot become faster or stronger in just a few days. He cannot learn tactics. Everything cannot be improved all at once for his performance and value to shoot up.

It's a broad scale and it doesn't only involve one player, but the total amount of players. One of them might get lucky in a championship and score many times, increasing his value. In the case of Leicester, though, an entire team was converted. The man who transformed them was Claudio.

In the modern world of football, speed, strength, fitness, mental stability, and agility skills are qualities that one must work on for years to obtain. All these qualities cannot be improved in only a few months of a football season.

What happened with the players of Leicester was unbelievable. At the right time and place, not one, not two players, but a whole team worked harmoniously together and offered something more. With positive energy and commitment to their goal, they went that extra mile in the name of English football and that was the key to everything.

When you're on a team like Leicester, the most you can achieve is to ensure that you remain in a category without falling to the relegation zone. The miracle changed the lives of Claudio's players. He passed the torch of his philosophy to them. He did not make any changes. From the beginning of the championship until the end, he kept things untouched. He used the same strategy, a specific strategy, a good defense mechanism, keeping the ball rolling at all times on the pitch.

The biggest bet was won when they were not on the pitch, though. He would talk to his players every day. There was communication and understanding. He was there for all of them at any given time. He was father to a bunch of lads who had begun to believe in the dream. Life was making it possible. He confirmed that for them.

Champions of England...it was music to their ears. There was nothing else in the world they would rather hear in their football careers than that.

They Broke the Bank

In the contracts of Leicester's players there is no provision for an extra bonus if a championship is won. Whoever dared to ask for such a thing would certainly be shown the door to the insane asylum.

The bonus that Vichai, the owner, would give the players if they survived the rounds was an amount of about 3,500,000 GBP to split between them. This bonus would increase incrementally for every place above 17th place.

They would split 4,500,000 GBP for 16th and 15th place; 5,500,000 GBP for 14th and 13th places; and 6,500,000 GBP for 12th place and above. The agreement provided that the bonus would be received based on each of their participation.

CLAUDIO RANIERI – T(H)INKERMAN

There was a fixed amount for each match of 9,500 GBP. If someone featured in all the matches, he would receive about 370,000 GBP. There was also a bonus of 3,000 GBP for every match Leicester won.

Unlike the players, Claudio knew how to negotiate for himself and for his contracts. When he was negotiating his terms with Leicester, there was only one term regarding a bonus: for any place above 17th—one place before the relegation zone—he wanted 100,000 GBP.

At the end of the road, when Leicester won the title, Ranieri was 1,700,000 GBP richer from his bonuses alone.

25

The Algerian Magician

Sarcelles is not the best suburb of Paris to live in, especially in the 1990s. The riots between the migrants and the delinquents were daily phenomena. It wasn't far from the center of the French capital, about 8 kilometers away. But from the 1960s and on, there was a ghetto established and many migrants who had fled the war in Algeria were living there. Life was difficult and there was no way out other than football.

A little scrawny lad walked the streets with his mates. His father had taken him by the hand and told him the secrets of football. In that neighborhood, in a little basketball court, with concrete ground that had potholes full of water, they would all chase the dream. Looking at that little scrawny lad, the dream seemed as if it would be unapproachable. He was skin and bones and there was probably no hope for him to ever become any kind of athlete.

But his father believed in him. He worked on his technique with him every single day. But fate can be unmerciful and his father was cruelly taken away from him when he passed away from a massive heart attack. Riyad's world dropped out from under him. He worshipped his father. His father was his hero. He was just 15 years old, and like many lads his age, his father was his rock.

Ahmed, Riyad's father, was a technician, who had played football in Algeria. In their neighborhood, everyone would be in awe when he would perform tricks with the ball, catching it at the back of his neck. Young Riyad wanted to learn how to balance the ball on his head, just like his father. His father was his football idol. He looked up to him. His father was the one who planted the seed for him to want to become a professional football player.

All the children in the neighborhood admired Riyad Mahrez. He could run circles around them all, one by one. He was a small magician with the ball at his feet. During his first teenage years in Sarcelles, the coaches would say that he didn't show much promise because he was too thin. He did not improve as much as he should have, especially in his teenage years, because he was not very strong. Unfortunately, there was not much room for improvement because the team would not give him the opportunity to work. He was never the first choice to play on any teams. He had something, though. He may have been weak physically, but he had heart. He had faith that he could reach his goal. His faith and spirit overpowered his weaknesses.

The truth is that even now Riyad has not shown any real muscle, but his sharpness in the game made him the best player in the Premier League for the 2015-2016 season.

Mahrez worked very hard, painfully committed to his goal from a very young age. Nothing was handed to him and he always told his mates in the neighborhood that one day he was going to play in Barcelona. After Leicester won the title, his name was all over the Spanish newspapers, which mentioned that he had become the Blaugrana's transfer target. Real Madrid wanted him as well.

Ranieri was the man who changed Mahrez's life. He trusted him completely and he gave him a place with Leicester. Unlike Pearson, he believed in his potential. He saw his capabilities in his technique and gave him the initiative to improvise during the games. He did not confine him to tactics and marking. He had other men for that. Kante did that with perfection. The Algerian appreciated his coach greatly and played his heart out for him.

His technique in the game changed the way Leicester played in the matches. He was calm and sure of himself. The way he executed and finished a play was fitting for football seminars. He was a hard worker during training and stayed at the training center until very late. Guy Ngongolo, Mahrez's previous coach said that when he was in France, young Riyad would stay until the wee hours of the morning training.

He would forget to go home and his family had to come out looking for him at the closed pitches all night long.

Mahrez was discovered by scout Steve Walsh in Le Havre. He brought him to King Power before Ranieri arrived. Walsh's past and agenda had several of the greatest players, whom he had discovered himself. Drogba, Essien, and long before that Zola was his real catch. He was respected by everyone and Ranieri knew him very well. Mahrez was written in his agenda later on as well, purely by chance.

When Riyad was 18 years old, he felt very defeated and thought about giving up. Thousands of kilometers away from home, he heard his coach from Quimper—a team in the 4th division in France—reject him. He was considered incompetent and would not be signed. He saw his dreams crumbling before him at a tender age, where things were supposed to start happening for him.

Exactly seven years later, he was declared the best player in the Premier League and became an example for everyone to follow. In the end his talent won and came shining through. Many new players start out with ambition to be professional football players. Most of them lose their way and never reach their goal. Their faith and conviction is pulled right out from under them. Mahrez is the best example. Never give up on your dream even if everything is pointing you in the direction of failure.

Leicester scouts saw him for the first time when some of them traveled to Le Havre to see Ryan Mentes, a 22-year-old winger who belonged to Lille. The Foxes were looking for a player for quite some time.

The first time Steve Walsh set eyes on him, he was very impressed with his technique and how well he controlled the ball. He could see that he lacked some defensive experience, but he was a real fighter on the pitch. David Mills, Leicester's chief scout, had seen him three times before Walsh gave him the final okay for the transfer. The 450,000 GBP that Leicester paid in Le Havre for Riyad were considered a massive risk and many people did not take this investment lightly.

No team had shown any real interest to acquire him. Many had spoken very highly of him as far as his personality was concerned, but that was all. He had his best season in the second division in France.

The Algerian Magician

Riyad has said about his team, "I didn't know Leicester. In France we didn't really know them because they were in the Championship. I thought they were a rugby club. I was like, 'I don't know.' But then I came here to see the facilities and they were good. I do not regret signing for them, it's the best club I've ever been at."

Up until that time, he had not done anything really earth shattering, but soon things became amazing. He went with Leicester to the Premier League and his talent began to flourish. The 2015-2016 season was the culmination of his football career. Riyad Mahrez's progress was like no one else's in the history of football. He captured the hearts of the fans and opened new horizons in the philosophy of British football.

Until now, we have come to know many of the great, fancy players who made the fans go wild in the stands. The Algerian magician, however, with his skill in dribbling, is adored by thousands of passionate fans. A ready football player who was perfected by Claudio Ranieri, who waved his magic wand in front of him and made him a frontline player, he gave his own account on his improvement to the British media.

"More experience maybe? More confidence, too. I want to enjoy myself. But now, when you're playing for a place in the top four, you can have fun but you also have to think of the team as well. You can't just be thinking about yourself.

"He asks me to be compact beside my teammates and then after that I can do what I want. He's very nice away from the pitch, but if you don't work hard on it, he's not! We have a good time, but we're at the top of the league because we run."

His partnership with Vardy really spiced things up for Leicester. The matches were more appealing. He was very sincere when he said:

"We just know each other's game now; I know how and where to find him, I've played with him now for two and a half years, so it's become much easier. But there's no competition between us. If Jamie scores then it's good for the team, and if I score it is, too. Everybody's happy."

Of course his words reflected upon the atmosphere that Ranieri created for all of them in Leicester's dressing rooms. Everyone had a part to play and no one was working against another. The team was one body and soul. Everyone had a common goal. There was no egotism, even in the most difficult of times.

Sometimes things did not go the way Riyad would have liked during the season of the title win, and that was when Ranieri was his tower of strength. When Mahrez missed two consecutive penalty kicks in the matches against Bournemouth and Aston Villa, the conversation in the championship revolved around whether or not he would continue to play like a star player or if the failure of those penalties would affect his performance.

Ranieri took it upon himself the day after they played Aston Villa to tell reporters that Mahrez will not be making any more penalties.

"'No, no, if we have another penalty, I would take it.' He answered me and said, 'Maybe you shouldn't take the next one,' and I agreed. But then I thought about it and went back to him and said, 'I'm going to take it.' He said, 'OK, if you're sure.'"

Riyad may have thought about it, but Claudio had his plan and it worked. When he spoke to reporters and said Riyad will not be making any more penalties, Riyad's pride swelled and he was back on track.

The 450,000 that Leicester spent to acquire Mahrez were peanuts compared to what another team would have to pay to buy him now. His story is a prime example for all young people who want to play football. You never stop dreaming, you never stop your efforts. At the end of the day, when you least expect it, the dream will come and find you.

26

Jamie's Fairytale

It is like a child's dream on Christmas Eve, where he dreams that all the gifts in the world are his and then he wakes up and finds them all on Christmas morning. This is a story about Jamie Vardy. An unusual story, a beautiful yet fascinating story that began with Sheffield and had a happy ending with Leicester, on a rainy April night, at his home with his teammates. They had all gathered there, the whole gang, to celebrate Tottenham's potential slip-up. Eden Hazard had not let them down.

Life was hard for the skinny lad and nothing was served to him on a silver platter; he had many rejections and hardships, but life changed for him and was absolutely generous.

His story is about the power of victory, the will to succeed in whatever you set out to do, and about being able to achieve great things, as long as you believe in your goal.

It was a known fact that Vardy—like most young lads his age—was crazy for football. They only had one dream in life—to become like David Beckham.

Jamie's Fairytale

When Jamie was 11 years old, his parents decided to enroll him in Sheffield Wednesday Academy; little did they know what would follow.

Many teams acquire talented players and work with them. Eventually most of them tail off, in a way, and stop persisting, others abandon them, and some may lose them because they didn't believe in them. There is no right or wrong way to create a player. There are effective methods that differ from country to country, just like the way the game is played differs as well. In Britain the old doctrine still exists: the young lad who wants to play professional football has to be strong and burly, and an accomplished athlete.

When Vardy first started out, he wasn't able to achieve great things. When he was 16 years old, he was released by Sheffield because they thought he was too small and would never amount to anything in football.

His first thought was to quit altogether since he dreamed of playing professionally and at that time it seemed as if all his dreams had been cast aside. It is not easy to determine at what age children have reached their football peak. But it is inevitable and obvious that when children are rejected at such a vulnerable age, they will suffer emotionally.

Many parents and coaches are quick to come to conclusions, positive or negative, about how a child will progress in a sport based on his physique. This is exactly what happened not only in Mahrez's case, but with Vardy as well.

According to research by the University of Murcia, in Spain, a large number of young football players abandon their efforts even though they have special qualities and the mental capacities to have a great future in football. Academies like great Barcelona and very popular La Masia both left an indelible mark on the history of world football because of the stars that emerged from them, not only from the way they trained but for their playing style as well. The players that were distinguished were not known for their physical qualities.

Xavi, Iniesta, and Messi had perception skills that were specifically developed to play football, and they became stars. They were not the tallest or the toughest. They were not distinguished for their strength. They developed the perception intelligence that a football player needs to be quick-witted on the pitch. The fastest thinkers of all become world class.

Messi or Iniesta's minds, compared to the minds of other players, had the ability to function full steam ahead when on the pitch. They got the ball quickly and passed it back and forth in complete synchronization with each other, gaining distance and power.

Young Jamie did not have many of the standard qualities other than speed, which set him apart from the others. His lightning speed was impossible to keep up with when he was in an open area, but he knew that speed was not enough and that he would have to work more in order to survive in the competitive and rough world of British professional football.

The coaches for the younger players were able to see his weaknesses, but they were not able to see how strong willed he was to reach his goal. They did not see his dedication and his energy. In the end, his strong spirit finally outweighed any weaknesses and made him a world-class player.

Jamie's strongest weapon was his passion; he wanted to prove it not only to himself but to the coaches as well. He wanted to show them how wrong they were about him. He asked to play for Stocksbridge Park Steels, a seventh-level team in England. He took a few steps back in order to pick up speed to take off and fly. It did not take long. He went up levels with the team and started loading up the opposition's nets with the goals he scored.

In 2007, when he played with the first team, they called him in and announced to him that he would be receiving 35 GBP per week. When he received his first payment, he threw an epic party for all his friends; they went to the cinema to see *Lord of the Rings* and he treated everyone to their admission tickets. The money he made from playing football was enough for cinema tickets, but it wasn't enough to cover his family expenses.

He had to work as an electrician in a carbon-fiber splint factory. The hours of his shifts were grueling and waking up at 6 o'clock in the morning wore him down.

A little bus would pick up the workers in the morning, and young Jamie would fall asleep while leaning on the metal bars of the seats. He worked until 6 o'clock in the evening and then he took the public bus to make it in time for football training. Most of the time he had not eaten anything all day. Sometimes he would eat at the factory's cafeteria, usually just half-cooked sausages and soft drinks.

He would go home exhausted at night after training and the only thing he wanted to do was rest so that he would be recharged for the next back-breaking day. Life was not peaceful. The pressure Vardy was under daily caused him to act out. He was frequently involved in squabbles or got himself into trouble. This was the reason nobody could even fathom that he would ever become an English football champion.

From his childhood years, he had a developed a sense of solidarity. This sense of solidarity lead to his conviction after a run-in with the police. He was forced to wear an electronic monitoring tag on his ankle. He was charged with assault against three boys, one of them even had to be hospitalized. He beat them to a pulp all because they had mocked his mate, who was deaf.

He was arrested and sentenced. He tells his story:

"A metal ring, like a shackle a slave trader would force me to wear, with a special chip that I wore day and night so that the police could find me anywhere I was, at any time. It was my medal of honor. Every day I had no life, I had to be home by 8 o'clock. It was hell. If the matches were far, I could only play for an hour and then I had to leave to make it home by 8 o'clock. A lot of times, we were lucky and would be winning, and then they would take me out. I would hop the fence to go find my father who was waiting for me in the car to take me home so I wouldn't break curfew. For six whole months this went on and I was in a rut, but I never gave up."

The scientific approach of contemporary reality in football—at least as endorsed in the big clubs of England, Spain, Germany, and Italy—requires rules, guiding principles, and behaviors.

It was impossible—until the appearance of Vardy—to argue that someone who is an amateur player at the age of 20 would later become a champion and be called to the national team of England.

Vardy was never a member of the big popular football academies where they pay attention to every detail in the creative phase of the football player's development.

In athletics, especially football, the results of training and the athlete's life are shown cumulatively. In order for someone to improve their playing level, a lot of time and patience is needed. The results are long-term, but are certainly not noticeable right away.

Talent is found among young people and that is when a plan of action is determined to work toward successful results. In the history of world football players, Vardy's story is unique. He was not the runner who suddenly broke all the timers after administering a substance to make him run faster. He was not the weightlifter who suddenly lifted ten kilos more for a world record but who had followed a "preparation program," as they were called, with a budget of millions spent on performance-enhancing drugs. He was a football player and his career would not change easily.

The drive to put yourself out there, the passion to believe that the impossible can be achieved, and the positive energy generated to reach your goal are qualities that you cannot get with any drug, nor are they based on any preparation program. Ranieri's role was the decisive one, and he was the one who masterfully inspired his strongest weapon by giving him the freedom to think and perform.

Claudio's inspiration and strategy found the ultimate interpreter out on the pitch: Jamie Vardy. Alongside the fully developed feeling of team spirit, there were a few moments during Leicester's magical season where Vardy had to run and pick up the slack and cover the errors and oversights of his teammates. He worked tirelessly, acting as a defensive forward supporting his teammates, even though by nature he was a striker.

Indeed such a phenomenon is rare. Until Vardy appeared, it was practically impossible to explain how a person could get to the top under these circumstances. When Sheffield released Vardy, he was going through adolescence and had grown 20 centimeters in one summer, making it impossible for him to move fluidly because his body would not cooperate for him to manage his technique. That is when he thought of stopping because he did not have adequate support to handle the changes his body was undergoing.

A mate of his urged him to carry on and since then the story has became one of mythical proportions. He came out of nowhere and became a shining star. Ranieri knew his story. "He is our Neymar," he would say, making Jamie feel like the highest paid movie star in the world. He gave him emotional support. After the game with West Ham, Ranieri had to calm him down. After he got the red card and was banned from the last important matches, he said, "We can cope without Jamie."

He treated him like a prince out of a storybook, but he did not differentiate him from the rest of his warriors.

When Leicester spent 1,000,000 GBP to buy him from Fleetwood Town, there was much skepticism and doubt about the four-division leap. It was the most expensive football player transfer since Conference and in his first season the 16 goals he scored helped Leicester move up to the Premier League.

It's the ultimate dream come true, which all people have when they begin to envision the future. You never know where you will end up and how much you accomplish. Messi and Ronaldo had the spotlight on them since they were children. Vardy wrote his story and his legend on the way, proof that anything in life is possible.

27

You're Always Talking

Jamie Vardy is in a class by himself. His story was not like that of other players. It is a special story and that it is how it will be approached throughout the history of British football. There are instances of players, who, through their performance and their days on the pitch, have left a permanent imprint in the history of football.

George Best was considered a football phenomenon. He was a legend. But he fell victim to alcohol and other passions. More recently, reports and photos of Paul Gascoigne shocked the British public as they portrayed him going around in public almost nude, with a bottle in his hand. Tony Adams publicly admitted that he too has an alcohol problem.

The tremendous pressure exerted by constantly being in the spotlight, often causes football stars in England to collapse under its weight. Vardy's statement during the season was a matter of concern because in the past he had some troubles due to his alcohol consumption.

"I can't say why I started, but last season I decided to have a glass of wine the night before every championship match. I am not normally superstitious, but from the moment I scored against Sunderland on opening day, I never stopped scoring."

He meant something totally different than how it was perceived, but he still underwent scrutiny for it and what he said was blown out of proportion.

Vardy had a tough time growing up. So much so that it is surreal that he was able to get where he was. He was born and bred in Sheffield at the beginning of January 1987. His mother, Lisa, never married his father Richard Gil. Richard occasionally worked, but he never had a steady income. He was not able to offer child support for Jamie and so he and his mother were forced to go live with his grandparents.

A little while after Jamie was born, his father had an affair resulting in his girlfriend becoming pregnant. It was inevitable that his mother and father split up. Jamie, practically a newborn, was left alone with his mother. His father disappeared and Lisa married Phil Vardy. Phil adored Jamie and raised him as if he were his own child; he even adopted him and gave him his name. Phil was the one who introduced Jamie to the fascinating world of football and was very supportive of him since the very first day. Phil always stood by him during the hardest of times, when he was rejected from Sheffield.

"When I was rejected by the team that I had supported my entire life, it was really a big blow and I began to think that football was not for me."

Very often in a football player's life, there are moments where disappointment dominates everyday living. Football can have more disappointing moments than happy ones, but they are such significant moments that they remain embedded in one's memory forever. Claudio knew about Vardy's troubled past. Their professional relationship did not always have happy moments. There were times where there were blow-ups and tension. Vardy mentions one of those instances in his autobiography:

"One day the Italian tactician got after me because I was talking nonstop; I just looked at him confused, and Claudio said, 'You, you are always talking. You are like a fucking radio! You, the radio whore.' The name stuck."

Jamie's life is one adventure after another. His marriage to Becky Nicholson caused a family feud. His parents did not agree with his choice. So the sharks seized the opportunity to busy themselves with the matter.

"We do not speak with Jamie anymore. I gave him 22 years of my life to get him where he is today, to have it all thrown back in my face. We won't be going to the wedding. We have not spoken for a year now, ever since she showed up.

"When Jamie was in trouble, and had a curfew, I was the one who would be all around the country to bring him home in time. It's a real shame and very sad. I have given him 22 years of life to get him to the pinnacle of his career, and I can't enjoy it. We have no contact anymore and it really upsets me."

Phil spoke those words. He saw the harsh reality of how success can change a person.

Jamie's maternal grandfather, Gerald, is on the same wavelength and has ill feelings over the marriage as well:

"It's because of that woman he's got. As far as Jamie is concerned, we do not see him anymore. It's a shame. I do not go to the matches he plays in anymore. I have never been to a Leicester game."

When was asked if Jamie sees his mother, his grandfather answered, "No, not anymore. You should go see that woman he's got."

28

Forrest Gump of Leicester

A cream-colored right-hand drive Mini Cooper is the first to pull into Leicester's training grounds and always the last to leave when training is over. If you didn't know who the driver was, you would think that it was one of the workers at the training center. The driver of the car was a goodhearted young man, with a smile for everyone whenever he would come and go.

Life has not been easy for N'Golo, who from his childhood was able to do something better than anyone else. He could run. He ran with his eight siblings and his parents, who migrated to France from Mali. He ran to escape the gangs surrounding the Gare du Nord train station in Paris, where he was born but had a very difficult childhood.

For Kante, football was the only way of escape from the sad everyday life of poverty. It is extraordinary that the life stories of Leicester's players, who were the front men for the miracle, have a common denominator: they come from a life of hard knocks, but by believing in something they were able to make a change for the better.

Kante's story shares many characteristics with those of Vardy and Mahrez. Five years before Leicester won the title, nobody would have believed that young N'Golo would progress so amazingly well, since he played in the eight division of France. Until he went to Caen, moving up to the first division—the ever-famous Championnat—he played for a while with Boulogne.

Steve Walsh, a scout for Leicester, was the one who believed in Kante. In the beginning, Ranieri wasn't sure if he should risk acquiring N'Golo. He had reservations about his height, which was just 1.86 meters and it was difficult to convince him that little Tom Thumb would be able to survive the hard Premier League. First of all, he would be in danger of being swallowed up by the warriors in the defense zone who were usually big, invincible men.

Leicester acquired Kante from Caen for 5,500,000 GBP, not a small price to pay for a player who did know now how to compete. When the season opened, the truth was known about the true value of the precious and rare football gem that had been discovered.

When Claudio Ranieri saw N'Golo Kante at Leicester's first training session, he whistled to the midfielder and called him over. He asked him to stop running up and down constantly. Claudio was amazed. He had never seen such a wonder. It was incredible. Kante could do everything: he could run, he could mark, he could play defense, he could play offence, he could pass the ball with ease in larger or more confined areas, he could cover the other players in times of weakness. He was a universal tool, which is needed in contemporary football, but which is also very hard to find.

When the Italian was asked how the Frenchman reacted when he told him to stop running, Ranieri, sounding defeated, said, "He turned around, went back on the pitch, and started running again."

CLAUDIO RANIERI – T(H)INKERMAN

When Ranieri came to Leicester to officially take on the team, many were skeptical about him as well. The first people to be skeptical were his new players. He said that they also feared his Italian mentality—which might mean he would take disciplinary actions in the same way his compatriots do—but they worried about his strategy of finding players for the team, as well.

Ranieri immediately knew what he had in his hands and built Leicester's suspensive operation around Kante. The Frenchman was the main part of his machine. He was capable of doing anything. He was cutting edge. He helped on the wings and brought the game to the center with square passes. He shared the ball exquisitely and whenever he was needed, he was on Leicester's attacking line-up.

At the end of the 2015-2016 season, Leicester's Forest Gump—the lad that never stopped running—became the bone of contention for all the top teams of the world. Chelsea was able to outbid and acquire him for about 30,000,000 GBP after the EURO 2016, where he appeared with the national team of France's jersey.

No one can match Kante. He was able to make his dream come true because he believed in himself. Ranieri showed him the way. He gave him advice on how he should distribute his energy on the pitch. He made him a first-line player because he taught him how to think.

A little while before Kante left the team to go play for Chelsea, Ranieri publicly asked him to stay with the team because he was very valuable to them. Though he was not able to change his mind, he—and everyone else in the world of football—knew deep inside that he had made an impact on N'Golo's life.

29

Morgan the Magic Rum

At each of Leicester's public appearances, all eyes are focused on Claudio and the ecstatic fans cheer at the sight of Vardy and Mahrez. But the one who steals the show only by appearing is Wes Morgan.

When the season ended and the title had been won, it was fashionable to drink rum in the pubs of Leicester and London. The rum everyone was drinking was not just any brand. The people drank rum that had the name of the team's captain. The makers of the well-known brand Captain Morgan launched a new product after the finale of the year and called it Morgan.

He was a captain as well, but his name was Wes. He never missed a single championship game with the Foxes. Morgan is on the label of the bottle, dressed in the team colors and became the company's strongest asset for their advertising campaign. The company decided to make 6,000 limited edition bottles, which became their bestseller within a matter of days.

Many rushed out to purchase the bottle that would be a souvenir to remind them of Leicester winning the English championship. When the commercial representatives realized that the rum was selling like mad, they began to think more seriously about promoting their line of products using Wes Morgan. They had discovered the best way to advertise their product and profit from the name of Leicester's star captain.

In every way possible, on all levels, and wherever they could launch their products, marketers would come up with ideas to take advantage of anything having to do with the Foxes that could be popular in the market. They seized the opportunity that Leicester's captain's surname happens to be Morgan. They found an authentic Captain Morgan, who was not just any football player, but the captain of the champion team of England.

They took a risk with their decision to change the traditional image of the bottle, despite its limited production. They removed the pirate that was originally on the label and replaced it with a football player dressed as a pirate. The social media was on fire with comments and posts that went way beyond the UK borders. The strong boy—who twenty years ago would cut in front of whatever came to into the defensive line of Notts County—became a first-line star, and his name sells.

Morgan had the same fortune that almost all the Leicester players had. From obscurity, he became world famous. His relationship with Ranieri is based on mutual respect. Many times mighty Wes becomes a second coach for the team on the pitch.

When he was 15 years old, he was rejected because his body type was not in accordance to the normal football player standards. He took the news very hard. As a matter of fact, Keith Wilson, his first coach and quite an outspoken man, bluntly told him, "Wes, maybe you should consider another sport."

Morgan the Magic Rum

Morgan loved to play football and all his dreams revolved around football, which he worshipped like a goddess. But after he was rejected, he decided to give up. For a while he did not play at all, and had nothing to do with the sport. Years passed and since he had been underestimated more than anyone else because of his large stature, when England won the championship, he wrote his story in the largest golden print on the largest page in the book of his career.

Playing 402 games for Nottingham Forest from 2002-2010 was proof that he was at the peak of his career. He could not have imagined what would happen next. In January 2012, Leicester outbid Nottingham Forest for 1,000,000 GBP, and they opened the door to King Power for him. It had already been decided that he was the next captain of the team.

Morgan is a real bull with a young lad's spirit. He wrote his own history in the Premier League, especially because of his ability to jump and intercept the ball from the aggressive opponents. He knew how to take full advantage of his unique natural powers. He did his Jamaican compatriots proud as he is the first in the history of their country to win the Premier League.

30

Ranieri Merchandise

In Ranieri's home town of Testaccio, the day after the conquest of the title, Leicester's flag was waving outside the Roma offices. It was no small thing for your life, your work—and your career, especially—to become known and appreciated by everyone, and above all by your compatriots. Claudio saw online photos and he was touched. On the web page of the Roma fans, everything was decorated in blue. The occasion called for it. In a neighborhood of Rome, near the area where he grew up and started to dream his first dreams and ambitions, everyone was so proud of him.

Within a year he had become a household name and he had become a marketing symbol for Leicester merchandise as well. A whole industry was established in April of 2016 and continued after that so as to commercially market his success.

The increase of Claudio Ranieri merchandise shares in such a short time is unprecedented and has become exemplary in the business world. T-shirts with his picture on them have filled the shops around the world. His majestic course has inspired the creation of products of which sales have taken off. Ranieri as a gladiator, Ranieri as Che Guevara, Ranieri as a Roman emperor, and Ranieri with his warriors are just some of the versions.

Ranieri Merchandise

They are literally sold out at King Power, Leicester boutiques, or outdoor vendors, from Bangkok to Japan.

Claudio was able to change the lives of the vendors who sold the team's merchandise around King Power. They too had been down a similar road as the team. They used to have a small income, mainly from scarves or banners. A prime example of the change that was made to the local community after Leicester won the championship is the pubs and shops in the center of town. A few weeks before Leicester won the championship, the city had been decorated in honor of the team.

Shopkeepers painted the inside walls of their shops blue, and others put up flags or even went so far as to change the name of their establishments. The pub *Dilly Dilly Dilly Dong* is quite popular in the center. The fans embraced the changes and preferred the businesses that changed their philosophy to get closer to the miracle.

An Italian company created a board game named after Ranieri and it has made a big splash. The object of the game is for the players to answer trivia questions about Leicester and move along the board, buying and selling, somewhat like Monopoly. The first person to end up at the point of the title win, who sells all their assets, is the winner. The box has a picture of Ranieri on it and children in Italy and all over the world can play the game and relate to the miracle.

A company designed a limited edition shoe in his honor, even though they have no Leicester commercial rights. It is a white leather shoe with a blue stripe, and on the top tongue of the shoe, there is a picture of Claudio.

The thing, however, that really was a hit in Britain and raised coffee sales extensively, were the cappuccinos with Ranieri's face formed in the foam. It started in an Italian coffee shop in the center of Rome, the D'Angelo, where Massimo, who is a die-hard Roma fan, wanted to honor his compatriot Claudio in his own way. He invented the Ranieri coffee that has been a smash hit in Leicester and London. The picture of Ranieri with his players in Peter's pizzeria has given ideas to many other pizzerias. They put different types of pizza with different names related to the team, like the Claudio pizza, the Dilly Dilly pizza, or the Foxes pizza.

In a Leicester boutique that sells the team's merchandise there is a product line called the Claudio Ranieri. There are tennis rackets with his picture printed on them, statues in different shapes and sizes. He is portrayed as a warrior, as an emperor, and as a general.

There are baby clothes and clothes for older children as well. There carry-on bags for every use with his picture on them, available in every color and size. There are clothes for dogs with Leicester's emblem printed on them and the words Dilly Dilly DOG.

Another thing that took the market by storm was the Ranieri chocolates made from white chocolate and praline, and the macaroons in the shape of Claudio, which are sold in different places in Leicester, London, and Rome.

The tattoo trend has really spread and a Ranieri Roman emperor holding a sword costs about 500 GBP if anyone would like to permanently carve Leicester and Claudio's achievement onto their skin.

Ranieri Merchandise

In the pubs in Rome and Leicester, many Ranieri cocktails were consumed. A few days before the official celebration of the title win took place, the city's university—one of the best in Great Britain—named one of the halls that they opened on the day of the parade after the architect of success, Claudio Ranieri.

The inventive Neapolitans went one step further in commercially using Ranieri's name. They made a Vespa scooter model named Ranieri and they painted it in the team's colors.

In the center of the city, antique shops created busts of Claudio and sold collectable coins for 10 GBP apiece not only as a memento of the Italian's presence on the team but for the title win as well.

Street artists create artwork portraying him and sell the pieces at outrageous prices. They charge more for the Ranieri artwork than for any other theme.

At the King Power boutiques, the player's jerseys, especially Vardy's and Mahrez's, are big sellers. Many fans that want to honor him buy the jerseys and ask for the Italian tactician's name to be printed on the back.

The product that flew off of the shop shelves after Leicester's miracle victory is the glasses like Claudio Ranieri wore. The Italian company that makes them saw their sales go way up. The type of frame that the coach wears has become very fashionable.

31

Leicester Crisps

Leicester is also famous for potato chips and the company Walkers is probably the most solid company that produces snack foods in Great Britain. Walkers were founded in 1948 by Harry Walker and was bought out by Pepsi Co. in 1989.

On a share percentage of approximately 56% of the market in Great Britain, they have made history with their potato processing. More than 11,000,000 bags are produced each day in their factory in Leicester where about 800 tons of potatoes are used.

For several years, Gary Lineker from Leicester was the spokesperson for most of Walkers advertising campaigns. According to data that is occasionally publicized, at least 11,000,000 people munch on the company's products on a daily basis.

To mark the occasion of Leicester winning the championship, a few days after Leicester's official trophy ceremony, the company produced a limited amount of collector's bags of crisps with Leicester players and Ranieri's picture printed on the bag.

The snacks disappeared off the shelves from the very first day they came out. Sales records were broken and now more than 15,000,000 British people were eating Walkers crisps every day, but this time the players and Ranieri were featured on the bags.

32

All Great Loves Go to Heaven

If a unit of measurement for the love of a team existed then the love that the Leicester fans felt when their team won the championship would be equal to a miracle. Whatever happens from now on, even if it means seeing their team in the amateur divisions, the love of the people has come full circle. Great loves move toward heaven when they come full circle.

Never in the history of world football have the fans of a team experienced such euphoria the way the fans of the Blue did the last two years. From the hell of standing still, to the paradise of winning the English championship.

A few weeks before Ranieri was crowned champion with Leicester, the Turkish television channel TRT World went to the Midlands to make a tribute to the team. During the interviews, the crew asked the fans to express their opinion about Claudio.

It was very emotional and Ranieri knew very well what he was going to achieve and how he was seen in the eyes of the fans. People of all ages, from different parts of the city, of different nationalities, were unbelievably generous toward him and filled his heart with words of love.

He was emotionally charged because he could feel how much the people loved him.

"I thank you, I thank you all so very much. This is beautiful. I do this job because I am very, very happy when I make the fans happy. I make sacrifices in order to do this and I love to do it. I thank you for doing this."

His love for the people and his genuine emotions are immeasurable and he showed the same love during his long journey with Leicester.

Guy Andrews, a fan of Leicester and a reporter, uniquely described to the *New York Times* what this team means for football, what Leicester really means and what the club stands for in the fans' lives everywhere around the world.

"When the rock group Kasabian gave a concert at Victoria Park in Leicester, in the summer of 2014, the singer and guitarist Serge Pizzorno went onto the stage wearing a shirt that said Les-Tah. That is the correct way to pronounce the city's name. The East Midlands dialect leaves out a few letters and the lazier clipped accent simplifies it perfectly. Kasabian formed in Leicester in 1997and was one of the few things that the city had to show for itself.

"Until Monday night, when the local soccer team, Leicester, won the title. This is of even greater importance because Leicester defeated world-famous teams with giant budgets. One just needs to think that during the last two seasons, Manchester United spent more money than Leicester had ever spent in its entire 132-year history.

CLAUDIO RANIERI – T(H)INKERMAN

"I am a fan of the Foxes, as the Leicester team is known, and have been for more than 40 years. I was born on July 30, 1966, a date that means a lot to the English football fans. It was the day England won the World Cup. My father thought it was a sign from heaven and made it his purpose to make me the next Bobby Carlton (Sir Bobby was the star of Manchester United at the time). Unfortunately I disappointed him, although that did not stop him from taking me to every Leicester game. So, here is the first lesson for someone who is not a fan: you do not choose your team, your team chooses you. If we chose them, we would all be fans of Manchester United, Arsenal, or Liverpool.

"But the first match I ever watched in my life was one Leicester was playing in, and that was enough. At that time, being a fan was not an easy thing to be. The air smelled of hot dogs and cigars. The fans were singing their hearts out; they adored their team and loathed the opponent. Of course, Leicester lost that day. But I was hooked.

"My team was smaller than teams like Midlands, like Aston Villa and Nottingham. But then there are the super teams like northwestern England, Liverpool, Manchester United, or northeastern England, like Newcastle and Sunderland. We never win the title though, never, ever. We played four cup finals and we did not win any of them. The last time was in 1969, where Manchester City beat us 1-0. The team was unlucky, that's what we would always say. In reality, the team just was not good enough. During the 1980s when Thatcher was in office, Leicester was one of the places that young people wanted to get out of as quickly as possible. But when I moved to London, one of the things that I missed was going to the stadium to see my team play. If someone kicked the ball too high and it would go outside the pitch and all the little kids from the neighborhood had got themselves a precious souvenir.

"When I lived in Leicester, there was a man named Bernard, who symbolized the city's unnecessary struggle. He walked to the stadium every day the team would play. It was a 30-kilometer distance. He never took the bus because he was superstitious about it. You would see this figure walking in the street, rain, shine, snow, just to come to watch Leicester be defeated by Preston 3-0. That's the way things were.

"The club's motto is 'Foxes never quit.' Every time we would lose we would sing Monty Python's song 'Always Look on the Bright Side of Life.' The rare times that we would win, we would remake a Christmas songs: Jingle bells, jingle bells, jingle all the way / oh, what fun it is to sing when Leicester win away.

"Now how does one explain Leicester's triumph this season? Many factors played a role: the correct mixture of talents, a fantastic coach, hard work, and more than anything the belief that we could do it. Today Leicester is a very different town than the one I grew up in. The city now has a mixture of cultures, the most mixed of the Midlands. And the rebirth of the football team encourages a sense of unity and pride. Maybe now, the younger generation will be motivated to stay in town."

In the music industry, a band or an artist can suddenly become famous with a great hit, but in athletics, especially in football, it is impossible for the status of an athlete or a team to change overnight so impressively. After Leicester's miracle win in Great Britain, Leicester set the biggest and practically overnight trend in the history of football, but also in world sports.

If one counted the number of Leicester fans, sports fans around the world, then it is certain that the teams from Great Britain have the most fans, since there are a number of traditional teams with many faithful fans worldwide. Leicester's club, the Foxes of New York, is perhaps Leicester City's most popular fan club in the United States.

Ranieri's and the players' achievements changed the everyday life of many people by thrilling them and giving them joy. The approaching conquest of the Premier League has created legions of devoted fans around the world. It was a nice football fairytale with a happy ending. Even in local hangouts, where you would find devoted Leicester fans, it was hard for them to believe what was supposedly coming up and that it could really happen. Below is an almost unbelievable story.

Amzel Hamni, owner of an Indian restaurant in the city, expressed the desire to give more than one thousand free servings of Indian food to whoever held season tickets after the team won the title.

The menu had almost everything on it and whoever knew about Indian cuisine became hungry for tikka masala, tandoori chicken, spicy samosas, tamarind with rice. The first thousand season ticket holders who arrived at Amzel's restaurant showing their cards would enjoy the food of their choice, since the owner had announced his intentions of celebrating the title win in that way. Shortly after the end of Chelsea's game against Tottenham, when it was now a fact that Leicester was champion, there were huge crowds outside the restaurant.

There were thousands of fans waiting to exchange their season tickets for a meal. The owner went out of his mind, as did his staff.

He hadn't taken into consideration that Leicester had more than 25,000 season tickets the year the title was won. Perhaps he had not believed in the miracle of the title win and became overly generous with his offer. If he had opened his doors and treated everyone that had shown up to a free meal, the outcome would be his bankruptcy and his restaurant would surely be closed the very next day.

33

The Betting Miracle

When the 2015-2016 Premier League season came to an end, the largest gambling companies in the world experienced a turn of events which was unprecedented and indeed would go down in betting history. The possibility of Leicester winning the championship was something that in the betting world was equivalent to discovering the secret to the universe. It was not a simple thing even for the professional gamblers to understand what happened the 2015-2016 season in Great Britain.

In the beginning, the possibility of Leicester winning the championship was considered a huge exaggeration. Everything that happened afterwards seemed like a dream that only those who have a vivid imagination could actually see happening. Gamblers who used their logic, if there are such people, would never have bet high amounts on Leicester.

Whoever had a crystal ball but didn't really know about football had hopes of going to the cashier window to get paid. The rest of the people went to the bookmakers and placed their bets, putting down larger amounts for the traditional teams Manchester United, Manchester City, and Chelsea.

The Betting Miracle

After Leicester's miracle victory, the logic that people used when placing their bets went to the dogs. It's something totally cosmic. According to William Hill, the world's biggest bet maker, the odds of Leicester winning the title was like finding Elvis Presley, the king of rock and roll alive, hiding somewhere in disguise so he could live another life, far from the public eye.

The 5000 to 1 odds that the bookmakers gave in July of 2015 for Leicester to win the championship sent the people who usually place crazy bets to the cash desk. Almost every week these looming possibilities for Leicester were decreasing as time went by and Ranieri's team was on the top of the standings. The result was a betting craze during the season. Everyone wanted to see the miracle, but very few people believed it could happen.

In the history of sports, only seven consecutive wins in one day gave greater amounts at the Ascot Racecourse. Similar yields have not been recorded in betting history. Some of the most significant ones were:

1981: When England defeated Australia in cricket that had been considered a surprise at 500 to 1.
1990: When the world heavyweight champion Mike Tyson was knocked out for the first time by the outsider Buster Douglas. The odds for Tyson to stay standing up in the ring were 42 to 1.
1996: A betting record with the outrageous odds of 25.095 to 1 in all seven wins of Frankie Dettori on the same day in Ascot Racecourse.
2001: In the final Wimbledon men's tournament, Goran Ivanisevic entered the tournament with a participation card and beat the Australian Pat Rafter at 150 to 1.

2003: The rookie Ben Curtis won the OPEN championship at 500 to 1.
2004: When the national team of Greece got the EURO of Portugal, many people said it was one of the greatest surprises in the history of football at 150 to 1.
2010: In the Copa Africa, the draw between Angola with Mali paid those who bet 1000 to 1.

When the yields were announced on the betting ticket the day before the opening of the 2015-2016 season in England, similar chances for Leicester to win the championship were given for aliens to invade the earth or for FIFA to hold the 2018 World Cup in the Antarctic!

Some, however, saw beyond the obvious. They risked it and, for the hell of it, bet that Leicester would win the Premier League. Champion Leicester cost the gambling companies between 25,000,000 and 30,000,000 EUR. For instance in Ladbrokes, 47 people bet on Leicester, even though it was 5000 to 1, at William Hill 25 people took the risk and bet on the Foxes. The biggest amount was about 25 GBP and the smallest was 5 GBP. It seems that the big winner was someone who bet 80 EUR when it was 1500 to 1, and became 117,000 EUR richer.

Finally, so you have an understanding of what 5000 to 1 means, just think: the odds of James Cameron becoming president of Aston Villa is played today at 2500 to 1, but for Vardy to win an Oscar in Hollywood is 1000 to 1. The odds of Elvis being found alive have not changed, but Leicester won the title.

In the world of people who like to gamble, no one ever takes these sort of things seriously. When the possibilities of Leicester winning the title were discussed, it was always just for a laugh after having had three or four beers. The companies would give better odds that the Loch Ness monster really exists or that next year in England, Christmas day will be the warmest day of the year. Leicester's title win is as surprising as us seeing Barack Obama compete with the national cricket team of England after he leaves the White House.

When the bookmakers realized what was going to happen, they started trying to reduce their losses. They started giving cash and buying out the bets that had multiplied mostly after November of 2015 when Leicester was still on the top of the standings.

An urban legend says that Leicester's owner, Vichai, a mighty gambler, won more than 200,000,000 GBP during October-December by betting massive amounts on his team. He bet that Leicester would be at the top of the Premier League standings during those three months. True or false, nobody can say for sure, but whoever didn't worry and didn't rush out to cash in their tickets celebrated with champagne in the end.

For the entire 2015-2016 season, gambling companies all over the world had to pay over 40,000,000 GBP to those who bet on Leicester, after every match the Foxes played.

A first-class example of what betting on Leicester meant the year of the title win would be the case of John Pryke. A betting ticket, which everyone thought was a lost cause, turned to gold in a matter of weeks.

John Fillan, a clerk in a department store from London, believed that miracles can happen and bet 20 GBP at the beginning of the season when the odds were at 5000 to 1. He saw the crazy road

Leicester was on in December, but just like everyone else, he couldn't imagine what was to occur in May. His expected profit at the end of the season would be 100,000 GBP. A few months before, though, he could not resist and despite the fact that the Foxes were still in the lead, he cashed out and pocketed the 29,000 GBP, which is not a small sum by any means. John was afraid take the risk and wait until the end of the season where he probably would have received 100,000 GBP. He preferred to play it safe and get the sure lesser amount instead of waiting for more.

When the BBC interviewed him and asked him why he decided to drop out and collect the money rather than waiting to see how things would turn out, he strongly expressed his view:

"The opponents have started to figure out how we play and they treat us differently. It would be dumb for me to wait and not get the 29,000 GBP."

The opponents may have started to figure it out, but in the end they did not figure out all the secrets of Leicester's game. Ranieri's squad won the championship and poor John lost a total amount of 70,000 GBP because he didn't have the patience to wait three months for the season to end.

Probably the most accurate story of rotten luck in the history of a gamblers belongs to Peter Brayne. He could easily have a place in the Guinness Book of World Records for his hard luck. At the beginning of the 2015-2016 season, he was inspired to bet half a pound on Leicester.

In the beginning of August and a few days before the Premier League opened, when the gambling companies show yields, many bet on something crazy and of course they lose the small amount of money that they usually put down. If Peter had forgotten about the bet, he could have raked in about 250,000 GBP at the end of the season. Fearful of his massive investment of half a pound, a week after the championship started, he took his money out.

In the first championship match Leicester prevailed over Sunderland with a score of 4-2. The hero of our story, Peter, realized that by pulling out his money and withdrawing the bet he had played, he could double his money. Bingo! He thought it was the right move to cash out and received the astronomical amount of 95 pence. He almost did indeed double the amount that he bet, but his bet went down as one of the worst in the history of betting.

Little did he know that a few months later, Leicester and Ranieri would win the championship and he, of course, would have won a lot more.

34

The Man That Changed Our Lives

People's lives changed and they changed drastically for the better, especially those who were involved with football.

A few weeks after the Premier League finale, BBC journalist Rick Kelsey did a segment on the subject. He searched and found people whose lives had been affected by Leicester and Ranier's success.

One of the stories that stood out the most was that of Ian Stringer, a reporter from Leicester, who lived a quiet and peaceful life, just like the team's course had been. He was an apprentice until 2012 and didn't have many possibilities of building a big career and becoming a well-known sportscaster as he had the unfortunate luck of working in a city which had a football team that struggled tooth and nail every year just to avoid relegation or to stay out of the danger zone.

Most days when he worked there was nothing really interesting. The results of the championship season were not good for the club and it needed to be saved. Ian did not have the luck that his colleagues had in London or Manchester, where they were able to cover the stories of the big teams and every day was brilliant and they were involved in all the intensity and competition. He did not travel to Europe for any championships. In Leicester he would very rarely interview important people at the stadium. It was also rare that a famous manager or agent of British football, or other countries, would go to see a match.

For Ian, the team became his real passion after he was sacked in 2012 from Radio 5 and he decided to follow Leicester, heart and soul. In ten months, football brought things that a lifetime of experience cannot bring. Ian is a prime example because of the way his life was changed after Leicester's miraculous win. He used to just speak about the team and the matches that were only interesting on a local basis. Now he has to stay up late every night and has direct contact with every place in the world, from America to Japan and from Thailand to Italy. Every day he speaks to journalist colleagues and exchanges information with them.

Every week he goes to King Power and sits with the football greats and has the opportunity to interview the stars, like Fambio Capello, whom he sits beside very often. When he is asked what has changed in his daily life, he answers very sincerely.

"Claudio is the man who changed our lives."

It may seem natural for Ian's career to take off like that because the team is directly connected with his work. Claudio and his players also affected 20-year-old Jake's life. A bartender in a Leicester café, Jake makes a little extra money every week by betting that Jamie Vardy will score. His bets usually didn't exceed the amount of 10 GBP, but he would have fun making bets with his mates. When Leicester started making insane progress toward winning the title, it was around the same time that Jake was looking for work.

Leicester's tourism rate increased because the team's results had put Ranieri's players in the public eye. Many tourists spent at least an entire day of their vacation time in Great Britain so they could visit the Midlands and see King Power, shop from the team's boutiques, and experience the madness that had dominated the entire universe.

The presence of an Italian, an Algerian, and a Japanese player on the team became the main focus of informal advertising campaigns for many tourist agencies because they highlighted the multicultural background of the local community and broader areas when advertising the trips to Leicester that the agencies offer.

Jake began to work at the cafe in the center of the city many weeks before the Foxes won the championship. Every day, he experienced the hustle and bustle of everyday life and the change that the team's victory had brought to people's lives. Fans of Leicester came to the cafe and enjoyed their hot chocolate. The menu now has extra items from Thailand. People come from many places, of all nationalities: working Americans and students from Holland have become frequent customers. The sales have gone up and Jake's work changed drastically.

The miracle that Ranieri's Leicester brought to the lives of people applies to people of every social status. Olivia Daugherty and Jenna Smith play on the Leicester City women's football team. They play on the team for players under 18 years of age and football is one of their top priorities in life. The 2015-2016 season dramatically changed the way that women's football teams were approached in Leicester. There were financial investments being made now. More people were showing interest in the women's team. The inspiration derived from the success of the men's team increased their motivation and made them believe in their abilities.

They are more passionate about what they are doing. The young women on the team believe that they can do anything. More young girls want to play football now. Everyone realized that they too can believe in their dreams even if they do not have enough money.

The vendors around King Power watched their sales climb the year of Leicester's miracle. Nicky Brown works at one of the pubs at King Power. The sales of the places that sell food greatly increase on the days of the matches. The fans' mood has changed and they now go to the stadium much earlier than they used to. This means they stay there longer and the food and drink consumption of each individual has increased. In previous years, the job could be done with eight employees and that was only on Saturdays. Nicky, a Leicester University student, used to work for a few hours at a catering service in order to make some extra money. Today he is the staff manager. The championship win changed his work environment. The number of employees increased to from 8 to 70.

Nicky manages the staff and now they work all week for Saturday's game. Success has changed the lives of these people and new jobs have opened up.

The University of Leicester is now one of the most prestigious. Almost all subjects are taught there and it attracts students from around the world. There is an increase in candidates who are interested in going to study in Leicester. The team's momentum resulted in the increase of applications by 700 from candidates who want to take classes there.

35

The Premier League Will Never Be the Same

In Britain, the biggest topic of conversation is if this surprise win can be the foundation for the team to grow stronger in the future or if it was just a magical starburst that happens every 100 years. This question cannot be answered right away because only the events that follow will reveal what truly occurred. There is information to be analyzed, though, about the differences but also the changes that Leicester's victory can bring to the Premier League.

It comes as no surprise that same five teams that fight to become queen of the Premier League every year are the teams that also have the largest budgets.

The season that Leicester cut the cord, Chelsea was at that top of this list with 215,800,000 GBP; Manchester United followed with 203,500,000 GBP; Manchester City was next with 193,800,000 GBP; Arsenal with 192,000,000 GBP; Liverpool with 152,000,000 GBP; and Tottenham with 110,500,000 GBP.

All the teams are shown on the list—with the champion being in 16th place—an incredible and extremely impressive aspect. Ranieri's Leicester needed a budget of 48,200,000 GBP in order to reach the top, while competing with a total of twenty teams.

If we attempt to compare the relative amounts—and the momentum that each team develops as well—invested in the market of players, we will see that during the same period last year, Manchester City spent 69,700,000 GBP to acquire De Bruyne and gave Liverpool 55,200,000 GBP to acquire Sterling, two cases for which the amount of money spent for the transfer of each player was a larger amount than Leicester's budget altogether.

So it is inevitable that the interpretation of the connection between money and success is impressive, and highlights what Ranieri and his players achieved when they ended up becoming champions. Never in the history of football did a team's stock market value and player value increase in total and duration in just one season. After the team won the championship, Ranieri achieved an increase in the resale value of the players, after the team won the championship, of more than 1500%—and in only just 10 months.

Another thing is that the players had not ensured a bonus from the beginning of the season for placing above 12th in the standings. The agreement in the beginning provided for an amount of 6,000,000 GBP, with bonuses if the team were to finish above 12th place, which had been determined at the beginning of the previous year.

Two of Leicester's players that have experienced an incredible increase in value and just zoomed past the value of the previous year are Vardy and Mahrez. These are the players with the most headlines and the players who became benchmarks for the goals they scored and for the total of appearances they made. They managed to score a total of 35 goals and 17 assists. They both rank in the top five scorers of the championship. They are absolutely productive and at the same time effective for the club's performance. It is remarkable that both of them together cost Leicester about 1,450,000 GBP.

If we try to convert and compare the money that the team spent, we will see that the money spent in Great Britain—and in Europe as well—corresponds to a medium-scale competitive player, not a first-line star. If we observe the reference chart of the most highly paid players in Europe, we will see that the amounts that teams have paid in order to bring in the great players to make a difference are disproportionate compared to what Leicester needed in total to reach the miracle.

1. Cristiano Ronaldo: 21,000,000 EUR
2. Lionel Messi: 20,000,000 EUR
3. Zlatan Ibrahimovic: 16,000,000 EUR
4. Thomas Muller: 13,500,000 EUR
5. Ezequiel Lavezzi: 13,000,000 EUR
6. Jackson Martinez: 12,500,000 EUR
7. Thiago Silva: 12,000,000 EUR
8. Wayne Rooney: 11,500,000 EUR
9. Gareth Bale: 11,000,000 EUR
10. Angel Di Maria: 11,000,000 EUR

Vardy and Mahrez were not main choices when they joined Leicester, which gives more importance to the fact that they were able to reach the top together with their fellow teammates.

For Leicester to include Vardy in the squad, they needed to spend about 1,000,000 GBP in May of 2012. The risk that the agents of the team took was enormous because it was not a small price to pay for a player from the 5th division in the English championship. The same thing happened with Mahrez as well, who went to Leicester City in January of 2014 from La Havre in the 2nd division of France. The value of Mahrez's transfer did not exceed 450,000 EUR, but even in this case, the risk was very high.

The differences between the high-level players and those who weren't able to ever reach that point lies within a single factor that plays a major role in football: detail.

All professional players are fast, strong, intelligent fighters. Many of them have great technique, but some stand out for their details—which usually have to do with technique—and also for their mental skills. The qualities make them special. They have something different from the others and they are considered world-class players because they can absorb and express themselves on the pitch to the maximum extent of what the team needs. They will be there at exactly the right time and place to help make a difference on the pitch. They will run ahead to either score or to extinguish any danger that a fellow player might be under on the pitch. When the ball is on fire, they can make magic happen and earn trophies and championships.

36

Graffiti for Claudio

The scene outside Leicester's training center is usually the same, especially since the end of March 2015. The team's fans pay no heed to the cold and dampness, and they wait at the exit gate for the players to come out after their training session. Vardy with his blue Bentley and Claudio Ranieri are the ones who usually steal the show. They are both the ultimate stars of the team.

A few days after the team won the championship, Claudio wanted to take a walk to the center of the city with his wife. He had not even walked 100 meters before there was such an expression of adoration! Everyone wanted to shake his hand and thank him for the joy he has given them. For more than an hour, the crowd would not leave him alone. He quickly returned to his car and left for home. Leicester fans swarm around Claudio any chance they get. He is now a legend for the city of Leicester. He is the new King Richard in the minds of the residents. Soon a main road will be named after him. A statue of him will definitely be placed outside King Power in his honor.

Richard Wilson is a street artist whose work is not exhibited at any London art galleries. He is still very well-known locally in Leicester for his artwork that decorates old walls and old

Graffiti for Claudio

buildings. These works of art cannot be bought, but are admired by all the people that pass them when walking in the streets of Leicester.

Claudio is an art lover. A large part of his earnings from his involvement with football have been invested in pieces of art. At his homes in Rome, London, and Monaco, he has some original works of art.

In October of 2014, when I arrived in Rome to interview him for the state-owned channel in Greece, the first thing that made an impression on me was how he had decorated all the paintings in his home.

Claudio noticed my reaction and asked me right away which one I liked the most. When he took me to his office to show me around his book-filled library, an incredible painting caught my eye. Its colors literally radiated around the room as if they were beams of light.

"That's a beautiful painting," I said, in hopes of learning the details about it.

Claudio smiled with satisfaction at his acquisition.

"That is Beethoven by Andy Warhol," he said.

He had acquired it from an auction in London. He spent quite a bit, but he was an enthusiast and expensive works of art are made for enthusiasts. From having Andy Warhol in his home, we go to Richard Wilson and his amazing graffiti works that decorate the streets of Leicester.

One of his graffiti works had a theme which portrayed figures that played an important role in the world of sports. The work that he did near the team's stadium had become similar to Jerusalem's Wall of Tears. It is the area where the fans gathered but is also a tourist attraction for anyone going to the King Power stadium. People like to be photographed in front of the painted images of Ranieri, Mahrez, and Vardy.

The Italian is the toast of the city and everyone expresses this to him whenever they meet him. His presence with Leicester went down in history when their team won the title. This alone will remain in everyone's mind eternally. Claudio played the starring role through it all and now his generosity is being rewarded with their love.

37

The Impersonator of Love

When it comes to luck, you make your own, and if your physical appearance resembles a celebrity, you may be lucky and your life may change. There are Elvis lookalikes all over the world, who keep his memory alive and maintain the rumors that he is indeed alive and kicking. There are lookalikes of Michael Jackson and Hillary Clinton. Conspiracy theories that are caused by the actors who portray real actors and world leaders abound as well. There are thousands of Marilyn Monroes on the planet with platinum blond hair. Most lookalikes earn a living taking pictures with the fans who adore the idols.

Claudio Ranieri has a lookalike named Alan Ascroft and he is nothing like the others. He has never met Claudio in his life, but he didn't want to make living taking pictures with Ranieri's fans for money either. He loves women and that's exactly what he used his talent for.

The uncanny resemblance that the Scottish ladies' man has with Claudio Ranieri was the reason he struck gold.

He used his resemblance to the Italian to his advantage and would impersonate him in public, but he would not introduce himself with the name Ranieri. He just let people think that he was Claudio.

He told the British tabloids that women swarm around him, marking their territory. As Claudio Ranieri, he has had intimate relations with 26 women. The electrician from Glasgow, who has been unemployed the last few years, saw his luck change overnight. He had so many rendezvous with different women, he could not catch up. After the championship, things really got hectic and he became a regular Don Juan.

Claudio's lookalike was the news of the day in Britain and the ultimate heartbreaker. All the women wanted to sleep with him. When he realized what this could mean, he began to speak with an Italian accent so he would be more a convincible Ranieri.

When the Sunday Sport got wind of it, he nonchalantly stated:

"I feel as if I have won the genetic jackpot. Whenever I go out for a drink women surround me. They can't get enough of me. I would like to clear the air and say that I never lie to the women. I never told them that I am Ranieri. They just think I am and I do not clear that up."

When it comes to luck, you make your own, a wise man once said. The Scottish bloke says the same and follows that proverbial advice by making his own luck.

38

Don't Bite Off More Than You Can Chew

The image of Gary Lineker in his boxer shorts holding the Leicester emblem at the 2016-2017 season premiere shocked many people. Gary was paying his dues for a bet he made the previous year. Like most people, he was a nonbeliever that Leicester, especially Ranieri, would be able to win the trophy. He was not the only one who openly expressed his doubts with an attitude.

In England, simultaneously with the events on the pitch, the game in the media is very intriguing, especially in this day and age where on social media everyone can write anything they want to judge and criticize what they see with harsh words and comments, which can sometimes cause havoc.

When Claudio went to Leicester, he had the leading role in the criticism that was dished out by the droves. Many times the comments were quite unfair, but the football world can be a harsh place and he knew that better than anyone.

Many people gave their opinion wherever Leicester was concerned but there were others who had nothing to do with the team. After the season ended there was not one person who did not change what they had previously said. It's better not to bite off more than you can chew with what you say or you will eat those words.

The day that Ranieri's contract with Leicester was announced, Lineker took his weapon in hand and wrote on Twitter.

"Claudio Ranieri? Really?"

"Claudio Ranieri is very experienced, but Leicester's is not the right choice. It is amazing how the same names keep popping up on the managerial merry-go- round."

Harry Redknapp was on the same wavelength and could not believe that Claudio had returned to the Premier League.

"Ranieri is a nice guy, but after what happened in Greece I am surprised he can walk back to the Premier League."

Dietmar Hamann was very sure from early on that the inevitable was going to happen to Leicester.

"I can't believe Leicester appointed Ranieri. It's a great club, great fan base, but I am afraid that relegation is inevitable."

Tony Cottee spoke in gambling terms and did not hesitate to put a nice frame around Leicester's former coach, Pearson.

"I am astonished. I didn't see this coming. Obviously there have been many people linked to this job, but Ranieri wasn't one of them. It is a strange appointment. They took a massive risk getting rid of Nigel Pearson, who did such a good job. To appoint Ranieri now is a huge gamble."

Don't Bite Off More Than You Can Chew

Robbie Savage proceeded with caution but did not fail to criticize the choice.

"Ranieri is a good manager, but not for Leicester. Great name, bad choice, in my opinion. Time will tell. I hope I am proved wrong."

Frank Sinclair did not avoid taking his shots, but he was the only one that at least had something good to say about Claudio.

"If I was a player at Leicester, I would be excited given the players Ranieri has worked with in the past. But his job is to stabilize the team. I don't think they are looking to win anything yet. If they can be mid-table, then Ranieri will have done a fantastic job."

Alan Smith had said that Leicester lost its spirit and energy before the championship had even started.

"Replacing Nigel Pearson with Claudio Ranieri can only be described as a huge punt. The risk is that Leicester will now lose much of its energy and spirit that had taken them to safety."

Michael Owen had predicted the places that the team would have on the charts. The people that did not listen were the lucky ones.

"Here we go again. The top 6: Chelsea, United, Arsenal, City, Tottenham, Watford."

A few weeks before Leicester was officially crowned champion, the nature of the comments had changed. Naturally. Ranieri had become a magician and with his wand was able to alter Leicester's history and the English championship.

CLAUDIO RANIERI – T(H)INKERMAN

Lineker admitted his slip-up and kept his promise. There were many that contradicted themselves and changed what they had previously said about Ranieri and his players. The first and best one to do that was Gary, who poured his heart out on Radio 5 Live:

"It is extraordinary what is happening to me. It is shocking. We are watching this incredible event with my sons. It is the biggest shock that anyone can ever have. I couldn't take my eyes off what I was seeing on the television. There are no words to express it; it is something that surpasses me. I see my team so close to winning the championship.

"I was very emotional at the end of the game, I could not contain myself. If you are able to live such things with your teams, it is something amazing. It has been difficult for me to breathe the last few minutes. To be honest, Leicester is in my heart and has been since I was a child. I followed them everywhere and I always have season tickets. We won the League Cup, but what happened now is surreal. It is really incredible. Even if you would have told me at the beginning of the season to bet even one pound on it to win 10 million, I would tell you that it is a waste of a pound."

Robbie Savage was on the same wavelength. He had worn the Leicester jersey in the past.

"This is an incredible moment, a night like no other. Who could have imagined? We have been through so much with this team and we have seen the team play low. Now we are the champions of the Premier League. It is the biggest accomplishment in athletics history. I don't think anything better has ever happened in the Premier League. It is incredible and we have made many people happy. I had many doubts about Claudio Ranieri, I didn't think he could do it. I made a mistake too just like many others, because he proved that he is worth it. It is a fantastic night."

Chelsea's captain, John Terry, did not forget his friend Claudio:

"Congratulations to Leicester. Their fight this season means a lot, especially when their main opponent is Tottenham. Of course, it hurts us that we did not get the title, but it is fair that Leicester is the champion. We will be back next season. I am very happy for Claudio because he made it 100%, he achieved a miracle, what they achieved is incredible. They gave hope to the lower teams. Not only is Claudio a good coach, he is a wonderful man."

Jamie Carragher commented on Sky Sports:

"I think there is no doubt that it is the biggest achievement in the history of the English championship. I think what happened is obvious. In the past there were teams that won the championship. What Leicester has achieved is to give inspiration to every football club. Anyone that follows a team, no matter where they may be, whether they are supporters or not of Leicester, they saw that anything is possible.

"Football is like a closed shop, it has the same teams winning every year and nobody would ever have believed that something like this could happen, but all this has changed the way people think about it. Think of what Leicester's win could change for football. Imagine all this happening more frequently from now on. What happened is an extraordinary achievement and I just can't believe that it happened. The first thing that has to be done in the morning is a statue of Ranieri."

Claudio always kept a low profile and didn't respond to criticism or to the dirt that was thrown his way many times.

When he was with the national team of Greece, in the beginning, the headlines of the newspapers and many columnists were practically indifferent and that is because everyone was trying to buy some time.

Claudio had realized that his contacts were limited, even those who were around him on a daily basis, like the EPO agents or people in the same environment. Some people were two-faced. When Ranieri was in Greece, they made sure to cheer him on for whatever reason they believed. When he left, they made sure to throw a ton of dirt on him and give him a bad name with information they thought they had but that proved to be just a figment of their imagination.

39

Buddhist Monks and the Secret

For many weeks, the acquisition of the private jet that belonged to the wife of Formula 1 giant, Bernie Ecclestone, was the topic of discussion in Britain. The name of the buyer that had to spend 55,000,000 EUR was never disclosed.

A week before the 2014-2015 season started, Vichai brought some Buddhist monks to Leicester from the Maha Mandop temple in Bangkok. It was like something out of a Hitchcock movie. What business did five monks have at the Leicester training center, accompanied by the team's owner? The British media went wild and hundreds of rumors circulated. Jamie Vardy let the cat out of the bag in statements he made to the *Telegraph*.

When asked what made the players improve their game, he revealed the secret that there were some Buddhist monks behind it. The president had brought them in from Bangkok. Vardy's words cut through the British football world like a knife. How could it be?

Some people pay millions for motivational speakers while others call Buddhist monks into the changing rooms and they are the ones that win the championship? Whenever Jamie wants to say something, he says what he feels and he is very earnest. He is built differently than everyone else. He reached ultimate glory after starting out at rock bottom, so he has no problem in expressing his opinion on the subject of the monks that Vichai brought to the team.

"Yes, I can tell you that the secret is the monks that visited us in the changing room. The team's owner brought them in from Thailand to bless us. They came in when we were changing into our uniforms before the match with United. They had some sticks that they dipped into holy water and they hit us in the legs and the soles of our feet. They didn't do it hard, but it was as if we had just come out of the showers. There was water everywhere. It's the culture of Thailand and we thank them very much for whatever they gave us."

While the monks were in the area, women were forbidden to be in the vicinity so the team would not be tempted. What Vardy said led the way to the dance floor. Monks from Thailand had arrived and changed the team's image in just a few weeks.

Vichai's main incentive was for the monks to bless the team so any bad karma would be abolished. He brought them in to have a ceremony in the changing rooms to bring positive karma to the team. The idea of it all seemed completely surreal.

Five Buddhist monks in robes sat on the bench and watched the team train. The British media went absolutely mad with the story. The photos circulated caused a big sensation. The madness started to spread when, after the blessing, the team did indeed have consecutive good results, especially when the matches were played at King Power. After the match with United, Jamie Vardy and David Nugent came out wearing Buddhist necklaces that the monks had given them and some people found it amusing. When they defeated Manchester on the same day 5-3, everyone was shocked and the monks had the leading role of the day.

The results in the matches against Everton and Arsenal were just as positive and automatically the monks were mentioned again as stars.

Phra Prommangkalachan was one of the monks that took part in the ceremony. When approached by the *Telegraph,* he explained.

"We can only offer spiritual support, we believe it helps the players to have good health, to avoid injuries and be focused. Whatever we do, it is they that must still perform well, so they can win."

The monks do not watch the games because they are busy in the changing rooms praying. When they walk through the streets, people stop them and ask for their blessing. In the beginning, neither the people nor the players were sure about their role. After they got used to them, everyone in Leicester is completely convinced that what they offer is legitimate.

"We all concentrate on a divine power and we have seen that it works," Phra says and everyone enthusiastically accepts it.

Come forward, all believers, it is reality for Leicester. During the 2015-2016 season, Buddhists often came into Leicester during the week and took action.

Claudio treated them with respect and did not object at all to their presence.

Although he was hesitant in the beginning, he did not want to ruin the spirituality they brought with them, and so he left well enough alone. Anyone else in his place—even himself as Tinkerman—would not allow for such things to occur.

The journey had begun in the 2013-2014 season and Claudio did not want to ruin Vichai's idea to invite the monks and take them back and forth with his helicopter. They blessed the team all the way to the title. They improved the mood and atmosphere of the team and flooded the changing rooms with positive energy. Vichai is devoted to Buddhism and he is considered a prophet in Thailand now. He managed to turn the team onto something that was completely unknown to most. This initiation became Leicester's support mechanism. The spirit of solidarity helped the players immensely. Everyone was united and focused on the goal ahead.

The Buddhist monks played a part with their blessings, making them contributors to the biggest miracle to occur in the history of world football.

40

The Magician From Thailand

On April 29, 2015, Leicester was playing in a match against Chelsea and their coach, the eccentric Nigel Pearson. We previously mentioned the incident in the press room after the match, when a reporter asked Pearson a question and Pearson flew off the handle, calling him an ostrich, silly, and stupid because he didn't like the question the journalist had asked. That was just one such incident in a long line of reactions that Pearson had. Leicester's owner did not appreciate such things. Other incidents had taken place in the past as well, where Pearson had behaved in such a way. He had once yelled at a reporter saying, "Fuck off and die."

The message that Vichai passed on to everyone at that time was very clear. His businesses had to function like clockwork and the team had to work perfectly as well without the balance being disturbed.

No one with that attitude could be part of the project he had dreamed of. Even if Pearson was the best coach in the world, such behavior was not fitting in the plans that Vichai had for Leicester. He had to be dismissed, and someone needed to be found with the strength of character that would be compatible with the project he was working on.

Pearson was dismissed swiftly, in the same manner James Pearson (Nigel's son), Tom Hopper, and Adam Smith were dismissed at the end of the season in May of 2015. Their dismissal was due to a scandal that had broken out when Leicester was in Thailand. Vichai had taken action very quickly then, too.

During a trip to Thailand to promote their collaboration with the country's tourist authorities, the players used their mobile phones to videotape their intimate relations with some prostitutes, embarrassing not only the players themselves but their president as well, who had arranged the trip. The marketing project that the club was involved in had been blown to pieces. The video—with racial slurs coming from the Leicester players in addition their lewd behavior—circulated all over the world.

As was to be expected, Vichai had to find a way to make the team professional at that time, distancing them from such amateur behaviors so he could achieve the dream he had for Leicester.

That fact that one of the lads who starred in the video was Nigel Pearson's son also played a significant role for the collaboration to be terminated. This was the last straw and Vichai knew what he had to do. He wanted to change the philosophy of the club by appointing a man with a different mannerism, who could cultivate such a philosophy. A professional who knew how to manage not just the team but the entire investment that the Thai businessman had made.

Ranieri had all the qualifications that the club owner's son had in mind and was hired as Pearson's replacement.

"The club believes that the working relationship between Pearson and the Board is no longer viable" is what the official divorce announcement stated, and the door leading to the upcoming miracle was opened. Until the story unfolded, it was a puzzle of unbelievable and unique coincidences that would be recorded in the book of world football.

The truth is that in the beginning Vichai did not want Claudio Ranieri to be the coach of Leicester. He considered him a failure from the time he was with the Greek national team and he was adamantly against the majority of opinions within the team that wanted the Italian to be appointed.

At one point, he openly stated his opinion on Twitter, and decided to stop going to England and to Leicester for a while. He left the team in his son's hands. His son was the one who made the final decision to appoint Ranieri to the bench.

Sometimes the younger generation sees some things in a different light, more maturely and calmly, even if it happens to be the son of one of the wealthiest people in the world. Absence makes the heart grow fonder and as time passed, Vichai became—as did most people—a great supporter of Ranieri. He did not hesitate to shout from the rooftops that his first and only priority would be nothing but the championship.

Life had changed for Vichai as well, who, after his success in England and Leicester winning the title, received the Royal Warrant in Thailand and is considered a prophet. In the near future, a statue will be created of him to be worshipped as a divine being.

The tycoon now holds a colossal enterprise in his hands, which he built up from nothing and has a powerful name on the football map of the world. Leicester's takeoff had reached the level that Vichai had imagined. The fallout from the blast-off would not only be on a social level but also on a financial level within the next few years.

On a Wednesday afternoon in March of 2016, an impressive helicopter painted in blue tones landed in the middle of the pitch at King Power. It was a day when no matches were scheduled and the boss used the pitch as a landing pad. Father and son Vichai had no prior obligations that day, so they were enjoying their time together. They went to Leicester to have lunch at Peter's pizzeria.

You won't usually see billionaires eating in a pizzeria, but Vichai is special compared to other tycoons. A simple man, always ready to surprise you at the spur of the moment, he is experiencing the team's emotional journey in British football. He has the leading role in a deal like no other in the Premier League. In the past he had flirted with publicity, appearing in the British tabloids, but their relationship became stormy. He does not want to bother the players so he avoids going to the stadium frequently and hardly ever makes speeches in the changing room. He trusts Ranieri completely because he knows how to do his job better than anyone else.

Vichai has fond memories from Chelsea's stadium because ten years ago it was the first thing he saw from the world of British football. He bought a suite there so he could watch the matches. Now, ten years later he is the champion of England with his creation, Leicester, in the same place. His suite at Stamford Bridge was on the same side where Roman Abramovich chooses to sit during the matches. Vichai knows all too well how to read the signs and he always prefers to be in specific places at the stadium. According to a Chinese tradition, the number 8 brings good luck and that is the number you should choose.

From 2006, he always watched the game from room number 8, until August 2010 when he did the colpo grosso, buying all the Leicester shares from Milan Mandaric. He has signs he follows and never changes them.

The Vichai family is a traditional family of Thailand with Chinese roots, and they own an entire empire of duty-free products. King Power is Vichai's company that transports millions of goods every day to duty-free shops in all of the airports in the Far East. He also runs Leicester with the same care and passion together with his son. They have entrusted the fate of the team to people they trust.

When they took over Leicester, their strategic plan was to maintain all the people who were already working there before Vichai arrived. The reason why was obvious. They did not want to ruin the family atmosphere that had been created, as people built close relationships working together on a daily basis.

Vichai spends his time between Bangkok and his home in west London. His assets in England increase substantially. In Berkshire he has stables where horses are bred for the sport of polo, and have been the root of many discussions about its quality and luxuries.

The move that changed the status of the club, and gave new life to Vichai's plan, took place in December of 2014. Jon Rudkin, a tireless worker at the Leicester Academies, was promoted to the first team by Vichai. The role of the football director, the guy who runs around doing all the jobs that need to be done, is quite nerve-wracking. Of course, he doesn't have the fame and glory as those who are up front, like the players and coaches. The unsung heroes, who worked with due diligence for the target of the team, and especially with the knowledge needed for this sector, worked for hours nonstop.

Steve Walsh and Craig Shakespeare were two valuable associates who worked for many years close to the team, and discovered some wonderful players. Vichai's big secret was the trust he had in the people who came from the club.

Rudkin was the deciding factor for Ranieri's appointment in the summer of 2015. After Pearson's dismissal, the president called him in so they could both work together on finding a new coach for Leicester. They knew that this decision was of dire importance for the team. The general impression about Pearson was that the team did have a positive performance on the pitch. The choices were specific; Martin O'Neill and Neil Lennon were the favorites over Claudio.

Vichai was influenced by his son, who wanted to see the Italian on the bench of Leicester no matter what, so he made up his mind and decided to hire him. Before he officially met with Ranieri, he went to Bangkok for the final authorization and blessing from the Buddhist monks. It was a decision of Withayaram Woraviharn and the temple of the golden Buddha. Many of the matches away from home had been blessed by Withayaram Woraviharn and Vichai believed that every decision should be blessed.

His involvement with polo matches—a very popular sport in Great Britain—did not secure great possibilities for a positive and safe investment. The royal family and the British elite had the bigger shares in the sport. But the two titles that were won in polo—the Queens Cup and the Golden Cup—were a good foundation to build businesses on in Leicester. The success with the football team one year later, however, sent the Vichai family name soaring.

They became an example of entrepreneurship, if one thinks about the fact that they bought the football team's shares for about 100,000,000 GBP when Leicester was in the middle of the ranks. Six years later, they were able to transform that team into the best team in the Premier League and win the championship. If one looks for a similar situation to compare in terms of entrepreneurship, they will find the closest example is Manchester City. Mansour bin Al Nahyan had to pay double amounts to win the title in the Premier League. Vichai's achievement is the prime example in the history of the Premier League. According to Forbes, Vichai is the ninth richest man in Thailand and he also runs King Power International Group, not just the team.

Recently, his effort to buy Thai Air Asia became the top story for the media. According to a financial analysis, Vichai is planning to broaden his business to air transport in order to increase sales in his business of duty-free items that the family owns in King Power; Bangkok; Suvarnabhumi, the new national Bangkok airport; Don Mueang, the old national airport of Bangkok; Pattaya, in northern Thailand; and Chiang Mai and Hat Yai in Northern Thailand.

41

Thailand: An Opening in Asia

On Thursday morning, the busy streets of Bangkok were closed off for two whole hours in order to greet the legendary Leicester team, Claudio Ranieri, and his warriors. It is a very rare occurrence for a country of Asia to close off its streets during the rush hour to greet a football team. Leicester's opening in the Asian market was unprecedented. Asia's markets have always been special for the big European clubs, especially those of Great Britain. Practically every year, teams like Manchester United, Liverpool, and Chelsea schedule tours aiming to increase their market power in Asian countries.

Within this framework, the player transfer market has been well opened, and slowly but surely the big clubs trust Asian players more often, in an effort to be better developed in the globalized market, which is now part of the football sector for good

A 35-year-old woman named Oi Oi, wearing a blue hat and T-shirt that said "Forever Fearless"—one of the team's mottos—was anxiously waiting for the bus with the winners to pass. Her love for Leicester and the triumph of the title win took her to a tattoo parlor, where she got a tattoo of the team's emblem on her arm.

Thailand: An Opening in Asia

Lin Nia, a 35-year-old intern at the hospital of Bangkok, had asked for some time off, as did many others, so he could greet the team when they passed through. They feel like Leicester is an Asian team, and they share in the joy and celebration for the winning of the title. There is, of course, another special reason for all of this, since the owner of the team is from Thailand and one of the great players of the team is Japanese (Shinji Okazaki). Both of them are the foundation of this great success.

In Thailand, Claudio Ranieri was greeted with the highest of honors. There is a picture of the team—in which Claudio Ranieri stands out—taken at the royal palace, where they all knelt respectfully in front of the king. The most respected, long-living monarch of the world also accepted Leicester as if it were an Asian team.

It is quite impressive to analyze what it can mean for an entire country when one team thousands of kilometers away becomes a point of reference.

The definition of multiculturalism that Claudio Ranieri likes so much as a philosophy of life found absolute glorification through a football team and with the great title win. The man who supported the entire structure and with his choices achieved a miracle is one of the basic reasons people of different cultures were brought together.

A Thai tycoon who owns the duty-free shops in Thailand took the initiative to lead a football team in England and he succeeded.

A Thai owner, an Italian coach, and players from different parts of the world were able to become partners, work harmoniously, and achieve their goal. They worked together and achieved the results they desired, but first and foremost there was honest communication and cooperation.

Ranieri's strategic thought and his capability could be seen after every game where he would analyze everything realistically—and many times cynically—but always humorously. He uses his humor in such a way that everyone understands that he has no intention of darkening the mood or what he says isn't blown out of proportion. The Italian tactician always explains the performance and behavior of his players, focusing on their physical qualities and the way they reacted during the important games.

He emphasized the reality of the situation in his own special way, which gave him the advantage of controlling things directly and efficiently so that it benefited both himself and his associates. He always acted with feeling and avoided voicing his needs and ideas publicly, preferring to analyze them with his warriors each time. In this unique way he was able to approach the psyche of not only those who were close to his team but also of those who were watching things progress from afar. He had created an atmosphere of affection and compassion that reached all corners of the earth. All positive energy was with him because everybody understood that what was happening with Leicester was not part of some strange experiment or a commercial operation. It was his passion and his spirit. His heart and commitment to achieve the goal. It was logic and the absurdity of the unachievable that fascinates people in all they see happening around them. He had a secret recipe, which he put in a magic elixir and gave it to his players, changing the recipe week by week.

He and his players were experiencing it all in a daze from their long trip to Bangkok all the way from London. The fans began to cheer and yell "Champions! champions!" and put flower necklaces around their necks, the custom in the Far East.

Wes Morgan, one of the main players of the team, could not believe what was happening to him because he was the first one in line to receive the fans' adoration.

"In the past we were welcomed in a special way. We have been to Thailand before but this is incredible. It is unbelievable and there is nothing like it. We are extremely proud to be here in Thailand and we know very well what it means to the owners of a team, who come from here, who the last six years have done so much for us and the whole team."

The English teams that chose Asia for investments have only been the big clubs for many years now. Manchester and Liverpool's fan clubs have millions of fans and sales of their products make crazy amounts. Arsenal has an official, organized academy in Bangkok that prepares new talents. For years now they have been enjoying the financial profits from the Far East, creating a market thousands of kilometers away from London. At the end of the Premier League, the teams tour in Asia so they can play friendly matches.

These moves were aimed not only toward increasing the teams' fan bases in Asian countries, but also to increase sales of their products in the vast Asian markets.

The appearance of Leicester, the new champion, increased the competition because of the new player entering the game. Many fans in Thailand changed teams and became Leicester fans because they were mystified by the fact that they were at the tail and went up to first place, and because they were rooting for a team whose owner was from Thailand. That is why the people of Thailand identified with Ranieri's squad.

Every fairytale that has a happy ending captivates people all over the world. Claudio Ranieri and his lads were such a fairytale. When Leicester players visited Thailand, they became one with the people. They participated in all the events and honored the traditions and customs.

They did not provoke any situation, as had happened two years earlier. The people adored them, the royal family welcomed them with every honor.

They managed to change the psychology of a nation that saw a compatriot, Vichai, winning and waving Thailand's flag higher than all of the British football flags.

42

Vichai and Leicester

People were talking about Vichai's arrival since he managed to rock the boat in England. There were many people that firmly believed the course of his career had been shady. It is not a common occurrence for the owner of a small duty-free business to become a billionaire in just a few years. King Power, Vichai's company, now has the monopoly on all of the major airports in Thailand. The acquisition of Leicester for 40,000,000 GBP in 2010 caused quite a stir in a league that has seen its share of extreme wealth.

Vichai saw a great return on his investment with the Foxes. Leicester's true value—based on New York City's Financial Intelligence Research company—exceeds 436,000,000 GBP today. More than ten times the amount Vichai had to invest in order to get the majority shareholding.

Such a business scheme has not been made in football in recent years, a move proportionate to Vichai's rise on the global business map.

It was not easy for one to foresee the Thai man's progress, and the amazing part of the story is that while the team was being made, he was also becoming a legend. According to Forbes, in 2016 59-year-old Vichai was ranked the fourth richest person in Thailand. The Chinese tourists boosted sales in duty-free shops at the airports. His assets are estimated to be worth about 1,900,000 GBP.

His relationship with the political regime of Thailand, especially the monarchy, is very powerful. In 2012, King Bhumibol gave him the title Srivaddhanaprabha. The world's longest-reigning monarch wanted to reward him for his charity work and also for his success. In return, Vichai hung a portrait of the King at King Power, Leicester's stadium.

Airports in Bangkok are the twelfth most crowded in the world. Despite the fact that for 20 years King Power was active in the airport, only in 2006 did he manage to secure exclusive rights to the duty-free shops at Suvarnabhumi Airport.

Former Manchester City owner, Thaksin Shinawatra, blessed the move and Vichai became a tycoon within a few years. His competitors accused him of making his fortune through his contacts with politicians, and that with the help of the system he went from being an average businessman to a tycoon.

There was a strong reaction due to the fact that, despite the expulsion of Shinawatra from the junta military, the man who was prime minister had helped Vichai not only to maintain his company but to also open new shops in Thailand.

He is the absolute leader and competitors who attempt to enter the market—specifically Koreans—fall flat on their faces in one way or the other. Tens of millions of pounds were lost in investments, buildings, and new projects, as they would always fall into a power system that only favored his own plans.

He is now part of the powerful elite as, in his own way, he promotes the interests of his own country, Thailand, abroad.

43

Almond Sweets From Mykonos

In the living room of his house in Rome, there is a photo of him and his wife Rosanna in front of the temple at Sounion. Years before Claudio was appointed to the bench of the Greek national team, he loved Greece and was extremely knowledgeable about its history. He is a traveler of life and his culture goes beyond the narrow framework of a professional coach. He is cosmopolitan and moves all across the globe. He has homes in London, Rome, and Monaco and not just as an investment but because he likes to breathe the air of each city separately.

In his hometown of Rome, he enjoys the respect of all. In London—where his beloved daughter and grandson, Orlando, live—he enjoys himself and relaxes.

Claudio Ranieri is a calm man, a scholar, and very positive. Brilliant and kind.

He rarely raises his voice, does not provoke, and keeps an equal distance in his communication and collaborations. He is fascinated when listening, but also tells stories of the legendary figures of history and the Greek heroes.

Almond Sweets From Mykonos

A true blue Roman knows where his generation comes from and is a devotee of the good life. His love for art is a given and he is often at galas, which have nothing to do with football. In his house in Rome, art work and classic furnishings dominate the space. Simple lines compose the decorating of his everyday life. His library has a grand selection and the photographs on the wall of his office remind him of the glorious past with Cagliari.

The paintings on the walls of the living room are like a small museum of modern art. When the door is opened, you see a goddess in the living, a portrait of Elizabeth Taylor, which overlooks the living room.

Works by great artists such as Andy Warhol and unique etchings of the war in Rome create a magical atmosphere. His home is in accordance to his own personal tastes and those of his wife, Rosana, who is one of the best gallerists in Rome.

Claudio worships the Greek islands, especially Mykonos, where he vacations in summer. He has good friends on the island and people who deeply respect him. His behavior and dignity portrayed in his everyday life on the island are exemplary.

Before I arrived to Leicester in March of 2016 for our interview, I found out that one of his favorite things are the almond sweets from Mykonos. I purchased three boxes and took them with me. Claudio was overjoyed and shared them with all of the staff that were with us at the time. With excessive politeness, he explained the origin of the sweets as his eyes were shining. Then everyone started asking him questions.

CLAUDIO RANIERI – T(H)INKERMAN

Ranieri may have left Greece with a bitter taste in his mouth, in the worst moment of his career—and many blamed him for things he was not responsible for—but he never publicly expressed the slightest negativity about the country, even if he was there for a short time. He would be the best ambassador for Greece. He never spoke derogatorily about the Greeks and keeps us in his heart, even after the fiasco he went through. This move shows the greatness of his soul. When you know who you really are, you harbor no ill feelings. You overcome any bitterness and try to go one step further.

44

The Thinkerman of Our Lives

Claudio Ranieri's example breaks free from the narrow margin of coaching and football, and is now a guide for everyone. It's for whoever envisions their future and achieves their goal. No matter how big something seems, even for a professional, Ranieri has changed that outlook and has shown everyone that nothing is too big and that they can reach victory.

When the Italian technician began his long career in football, it was not an easy road. Many times the signs might be pointing to show us the way, but the ability to pass any obstacles in our path will depend on how you handle each one separately.

With the miracle of Leicester, Claudio fully proved that David can beat Goliath when he has faith and commitment and concentrates on the goal at hand.

For Ranieri's efforts in achieving his goal of winning the championship, the moral of the story is that the poor man can beat the wealthy man. The weaker man can grow strong and pulverize the stronger one.

After Leicester won the championship, many sought to analyze the event, trying to reach some sort of conclusion of how it was made possible. They wrote about strategy and the ability of the Italian to read his players, about the way Leicester operated and the way he did not completely change the team and trusted the same players the previous coach had. Ranieri's success with Leicester is a revolution in the world of football.

Scientific developments in recent years have created an industry of technological perfection. All coaches around the world apply advanced fitness practices and training for their athletes. Each year, the big clubs spend millions to acquire the latest machinery, which will give something extra for the ultimate preparation of the athletes. Each time, dozens of members of the training staff process even the smallest detail and any information that may be useful.

Ranieri succeeded in going one step further and added the human aspect to technology—faith in achieving the goal and his positive energy.

Leicester's scientific staff had some of the most modern tools to work with. It would be absurd to claim that Leicester was technologically lacking on an infrastructure level compared to its major rivals. On the contrary, Claudio was fortunate enough to have excellent partners beside him, equipped with the latest means. He trusted them, but what made the difference was the management of all the people.

Ranieri counted more on his life experience and less on his coaching knowledge, and he succeeded. He put what he learned out on the pitches first and incorporated it with everyday life and his players. For this reason, he is a life example for all, especially now that the crisis of values plague societies. He worked outside of stereotypes, he gave his players days off, he covered his players

The Thinkerman of Our Lives

when they did not perform well, and he stayed up nights to watch the opponent, to discover things with his own eyes.

At age 64, he was a fervent devotee of tactics. With many of the teams he worked with this passion—being a product of an Italian football academy—he paid for it dearly. In Leicester he quickly realized that his tools would not give him the opportunity to experiment and he left aside complicated tactics and systems. Leicester was totally predictable in game play from the first day, but no one was able to decipher and intercept how they played.

They played bad football, but no one remembers that because at the sight of the champion trophy, everything was forgotten. Claudio was completely honest and at the same time respectable with everyone from the first moment. He never gave false hope to anyone and even though he knew that most of them on the team did not want him there from the beginning, he showed how big-hearted he was; in the moment of the massive achievement, he was humble and did not blame or judge anyone.

He went through difficult moments during the season, but he ended up being a great example for all. When you fight and work—even when dirty games are played to deprive you of happiness—when your time comes to shine, you have to be twice as humble and modest.

He paid special attention to people around him and treated all his colleagues like human beings and not machines. All of his players were highly paid professionals that related to the expensive world of the Premier League. Claudio had to manage them accordingly, in order for them to believe in themselves and that is what boosted them. He freed them to the ultimate degree.

CLAUDIO RANIERI – T(H)INKERMAN

He allowed Vardy to move wherever he wanted to and allowed Mahrez to do his tricks with the opponents. He asked Kante to run wherever and however he wanted. He watched Schmeichel entertain the fans and smiled meaningfully. He asked Okazaki to be the soldier in several games, without rotating, and sacrificed players with talent in the name of team spirit.

This is the way his whole philosophy was put forth from beginning to end. He forbade Vardy to work hard during the week and sent him to the changing room first in order to protect him. When the players asked him to reduce training that included tactical exercises, he immediately obliged. Each training session was fun and everyone trained with enthusiasm. He even managed to make a pun about Morgan's extra weight, and every time he wanted to tease someone, he would always say it in a pleasant and humorous way.

Ranieri succeeded because he took responsibility for his actions every moment, from the day he set foot in King Powers. He would make fun of himself and kept his head up throughout any difficulties. He always backed up his players and never tried to make cheap excuses about why they lost.

He showed devotion to his work and methods, and radically changed his philosophy. This change was not due to personal defeat, but an effort for personal improvement. When he succeeded, his attitude and behavior was legendary. He managed the league title better after having previously failed and his reactions were unique. With calmness and solemnity, respect and discipline, he made his passion productive and transferred this philosophy to his immediate associates.

The Thinkerman of Our Lives

Shortly before the sweetest press conference of his life—immediately after the conquest of the English Championship—Fuchs and Schmeichel, Claudio's favorite players, entered the room holding the trophy. In their arms, the reward for Ranieri's lifetime effort.

Many believed that this sudden entrance by Fuchs and Schmeichel with the trophy in their arms would be a nice touch for the television crews. Photographers let the images speak for themselves, with the Championship Cup in the background and Ranieri speaking to the reporters in the interview of their lifetimes. Claudio's relationship with the reporters throughout his career was passionate one.

Casper Schmeichel hugged the Cup and placed it on the table where Claudio was sitting. Fuchs was standing behind him and started to empty a five-liter bottle of champagne on his head, completely soaking him. Everyone in the room froze. This was not the locker room nor the pitch, for them to be acting like children. This was the press room, in the presence of all the television and film crews.

In America, it's very common to pour a barrel of water over the coach's head when winning the title. The difference is that the custom takes place on the playing field and is part of the celebration once the match is over.

Fuchs emptied the whole bottle all over Ranieri's expensive suit. Ranieri was shocked, which was something that everyone could understand, but he remained completely calm. At this point he showed the greatness of his soul. He did not get aggravated nor did he react harshly. Some wrote the next day that he could have reacted but he didn't.

He politely let it be understood that Fuch's actions were not acceptable and were at the wrong place at the wrong time. It was the wrong place to celebrate like that because the room was intended for another purpose. His reaction completely overshadowed any negative opinion that one might have had for his players. He did not make a fool of himself by having a water fight with his players in the press room. He discreetly asked for a tissue to wipe his glasses and made a humorous and sarcastic comment about his expensive suit.

Surely no player of Sir Alex Ferguson's would dare think of doing such a thing. Jose Mourinho does not give his players the room to even fathom it. A few reporters felt that the players did not show him the appropriate respect.

Harsh words were written that criticized the players' behavior, saying they undermined him and that it was something he did not deserve, especially after the grand conquest of the Championship Cup.

They even went so far as to say that the players' conduct made him look bad at the end of the season. But Claudio's reaction was a life lesson for all. Mourinho would have reacted and reciprocated in some way. Arsene Wenger would never have the chance to experience something like that due to his quiet nature.

The conclusion is that respect is not something to be demanded, it is earned. Ranieri not only earned respect from all in Leicester due to his success in 2015-2016, but also due to his character. His stance and attitude during the incident was exemplary to all.

The Thinkerman of Our Lives

The lights at King Power had been turned off and Claudio was walking toward his favorite black jeep that was in the parking, so he could drive home.

The cries of the Leicester fans echoed in his ears like a harmonious melody in tune with his friend Bocelli's voice.

Ranieri made history as one of the best of the best. He opened roads that previously were inaccessible. In modern football, the role of coach has become that of the leading man. Before, coaches would teach their players how to play football; today, they show them how to work.

Coaches are like skydivers, not knowing whether or not their parachutes will open every time they jump into a new adventure.

Ranieri traveled the skies.

CREDITS

Design and Layout
Cover Design: Annika Naas
Interior Design: Annika Naas
Layout: Amnet

Images
Cover Image: grafima, www.grafimaprint.gr
Interior Photos: pp. 123-128: Aris Gatas
pp. 76, 156, 160-177: copyright by respective owner and used under fair use rule under 17 USC 107 and fair dealing UK.

Editorial
Managing Editor: Elizabeth Evans
Copyeditor: Anne Rumery

Subscribe to our newsletter at **www.m-m-sports.com**

MORE GREAT SOCCER TITLES

Luciano Wernicke

WHY IS SOCCER PLAYED ELEVEN AGAINST ELEVEN?

EVERYTHING YOU NEED TO KNOW ABOUT SOCCER

Why Is Soccer Played Eleven Against Eleven? reveals one hundred facts of soccer history and rules that are either unknown or little known, such as why soccer is played eleven against eleven, why soccer matches last 90 minutes, who the first coach was, how the referee appeared, and who invented goal nets, red and yellow cards, the penalty, and the penalty shoot-out. Included in this book are funny and weird anecdotes, such as the case of a player who scored a goal...without ever having stepped on the pitch, making this book is the complete resource on the game of soccer.

Millions of soccer fans will find all the answers to any question they could possibly have—including those they may not have thought of—in this amusing, yet informative, book by journalist, Luciano Wernicke.

ISBN: 9781782551379
256 p., b/w, 30 photos
paperback, 5.5" x 8.5"
$14.95 US/£11.95 UK

All information subject to change © Adobe Stock

FROM MEYER & MEYER SPORT

Alejandro Pérez

MORE THAN 90 MINUTES
ANALYZING SUCCESS IN EUROPEAN CLUB SOCCER

More than Ninety Minutes is an analysis of tactics, signings, managers, players, and club directors' decisions. Based on real examples taken from recent soccer history, the author dissects these people's mistakes, their successes, and how their actions on and off the pitch impacted their play and their trophy cabinets. It is a critical account arising from a weekly study made over the course of ten years of the top European leagues and clubs. The author presents and compares the processes followed by these teams—the ones that were successful as well as those that failed—while analytically assessing the most important aspects that make up the game of soccer. Without claiming to find a nonexistent magic formula, it helps the reader—whether they are simply a fan, manager, player, or director—to understand the intricacies of this complex sport. This book is one of a kind in the history of soccer literature.

ISBN: 9781782551225
300 p., b/w
paperback, 5.5" x 8.5"
$14.95 US/£12.95 UK

MEYER & MEYER Sport
Von-Coels-Str. 390
52080 Aachen
Germany

Phone +49 02 41 - 9 58 10 - 13
Fax +49 02 41 - 9 58 10 - 10
E-Mail sales@m-m-sports.com
E-Books www.m-m-sports.com

All books available as E-books.

MEYER & MEYER SPORT